Astrological Anthology

Frances Sakoian
and
Louis S. Acker

ISBN-10: 0-86690-658-4
ISBN-13: 978-0-86690-658-6

Cover Design: Jack Cipolla

Published by:
American Federation of Astrologers, Inc.
6535 S. Rural Road
Tempe, AZ 85283

www.astrologers.com

Books by Frances Sakoian and Louis S. Acker

Decanates and Duads

The Inconjunct: Natal and Transiting Aspects

The Transiting Planets

Transits Simplified

iv

Contents

CHAPTER ONE

The Importance of Mercury in the Horoscope

It is the opinion of many experienced astrologers that Mercury—along with the Sun, Moon, and Ascendant—is one of the strongest and most powerful indicators of the native's fundamental character and destiny.

It is generally agreed that the fundamental characteristic that distinguishes man from all other species is his ability to think, to reason, to remember, to plan, and to use tools. All of these characteristics are under the rulership of the planet Mercury.

The Mercury-ruled sign of Gemini governs the hands and arms, which are singularly responsible in distinguishing man from the rest of the animal kingdom in that they enable him alone to control his physical environment through the use of tools. Mercury also rules the brain and the nervous system, the character of which similarly distinguishes man from all other species. Mercury is therefore synonymous with those faculties that are distinctly human.

The fundamental psychological characteristic of Mercury is the ability to know, to deduce, and to use facts in an impartial and impersonal way. To this state of consciousness, the only thing of real importance is the truth, rather than prejudice.

Because facts are gathered through the senses and because the senses are linked to the brain through the nervous system, Mercury has a general rulership over the senses as well. People with exceptionally good eyesight, touch, feeling, or sense of smell are apt to have a good Mercury.

Only the principle of the Sun representing the will or power potential, working through the faculty of attention, stands above Mercury or the mind, guiding it and using it. The will (represented by the Sun) through guiding the attentions, determines what the mind dwells upon or entertains; thus it is creative in the realm of thought. The mind itself (ruled by Mercury) is said to be neutral and is therefore capable of entertaining any thought, be it high or low or pertaining to any area of human experience or knowledge. For this reason, the way a person thinks (as represented by his or her Mercury) is predominately colored by the nature of the planet that makes the closest major aspect to Mercury and by the sign and house position of Mercury.

The foregoing are the determining factors of the manner of expression and practical affairs with which the native is generally occupied. For instance, a person whose Mercury is in the seventh house would be largely mentally occupied with thoughts about marriage, partnerships, and public relations.

The mind is the creator of our destiny, so people are not in control of their destiny until they are in control of their mind. It is for this reason that mental self-discipline is the most important discipline in life. But how is it to be achieved?

The ultimate key to the matter is in the use of the faculty of attention. The mind, like a radio transmitter and receiver, is capable of tuning in, amplifying, and transmitting any thought.

According to the nature of these thoughts, people are emotionally and physically motivated into the actions and experiences that in turn make up their destiny and future karma.

Therefore, it is of supreme importance to wisely select and to be on guard concerning what thoughts pass the discriminating bar of the mind.

This is true because people have free will to select that which they wish to think and dwell on. Such a selection must be wisely made and careful consideration must be given to the probable outcome of any thought if put into action and communicated to others. If this is not done, disaster and personal unhappiness, coupled with failure, may be the result. For this reason we must constantly use the "I AM" principle in us, or pure consciousness, which is also the faculty of attention.

One must constantly observe the thoughts that enter the mind, first recognizing them for what they are and then discarding those that are negative, destructive, superfluous, or impractical. One must select only those thoughts that serve a useful and constructive purpose for further examination, work, exploration, and planning. This discipline, when practiced with devotion and serious intent, forms the true basis of religion, science, and philosophy—the only forces that can elevate man above war, disaster, and chaos.

If the faculty of Mercury is used correctly, the actions arising from Venus will be automatically directed into constructive channels, building up solid accomplishments for physical security and good social relationships, where love and human brotherhood will find its true expression. This is merely to say that the mind must, and can, be the wise governing principle for the powerful forces of the emotions—the motivating principles of life that give man the desire to live and to achieve fulfillment.

The emotions (which fuel the engine of man's life), when out of control, burn up man's vehicle and run him amok. Only through Mercury can the emotions be correctly guided and channeled into constructive expression.

The mind is not the highest of man's faculties because it is superseded by intuition, which comes from the Self or the eternal spiritual nature. However, in a practical way the mind is of equal necessity to the Spirit because without it the Spirit cannot control man's emotional and physical nature and cannot incarnate its expression in the flesh. The mind (ruled by Mercury) is the focusing lens between man's higher and lower nature, thus making possible communication between the two.

The promise of any natal horoscope can be brought into manifestation only insofar as Mercury provides the intelligence, communicating ability, knowledge, and understanding to do so. Therefore, a person (especially in today's world) is not capable of achieving great heights of reputation, power, or wealth if Mercury is weak and debilitated in the horoscope. Even if the native has all the other necessary ingredients for success, they will be unexpressed and dormant without the power of the mind to make use of them.

Mercury indicates a native's ability to learn and be educated. Knowledge and education are the most essential ingredients for success in our modern world. A person's profession is determined primarily by what kind of education he or she has and by how extensive it is, whether it be higher education or practical experience. In turn, a person's standard of living is determined by profession, as are the social contacts that shape his or her life, destiny, and experience. Therefore, we must look to Mercury as well as the tenth house and Saturn to determine a person's station and importance in life.

Inheritance of wealth can mean greater educational opportunities and be important to social position and station in life; but these factors will become less important as civilization advances.

Mercury, which also rules Virgo and the sixth house (work and service) is closely linked to a person's work and profession.

Since success depends upon human cooperation and since cooperation depends on communication (ruled by Gemini and the third house), Mercury here also plays an all-important role. Ideas form the mold for future action that creates the human reality; and therefore, the person who can formulate and communicate ideas precisely, systematically, and clearly has power over the future and can influence the policy of groups and organizations, both large and small.

This is seen in our country in the immense power of the mass media to mold public opinion and to influence government policy. This is why in mundane astrology the media, be it the press, radio, or television, is ruled by Mercury and also by Uranus, which rules the technical electronic aspect of it. (It has been our observation that scientists, while they may have strong Mars, Saturn, Uranus, Venus, and Pluto tendencies, will invariably have a well-developed Mercury.)

Mercury Links to Other Planets

Mercury as the ruler of Gemini is the idea planet. When Mercury is closely linked to Saturn, and sometimes when it is linked to Venus, a good mathematical mind is the result. This is because Venus deals with form, structure, and proportion. Saturn adds discipline, systematic method, and focusing ability to the mind. The Saturn discipline gives the capacity for systematic, sustained effort, which enables the native to excel at mathematics. A perfect example is Einstein, who had Mercury conjunct Saturn in the sign of new beginnings, Aries. He is famous for his pioneering of new concepts in atomic physics.

When Mercury is linked with Venus, musical talent and grace of expression in writing and speech are manifest. The native's grace and diplomacy make him or her skillful in a public relations role. Charm makes it easy for other people to accept the native's ideas.

When Mercury is linked with Mars we have an energetic, ambitious, enterprising mind, bent on success and practical achievement. However, there is a danger of aggressive mental attitudes, a know-it-all complex, and an argumentative nature. A mental competitiveness could result in prejudice in some matters; therefore, these people should strive for impartial and impersonal judgment.

When Mercury is linked with Jupiter, the mind is used to carry out benevolent and expansive social goals. The native is apt to be a promoter in some manner, whether as a businessperson selling commercial products or as an expounder of a political or religious philosophy. The native is mentally concerned about and occupied with the larger society in which he or she lives. Since Jupiter also rules institutions of higher learning and since Jupiter is a socially-conscious planet, people with strong Mercury-Jupiter contacts will be found in fields of teaching, journalism, and writing. These natives are also apt to travel a great deal at some time in life; this is because the mind is fed by experiences, while traveling increases the variety and scope of the experiences.

When Mercury is linked with Uranus, the mind is capable of receiving information from faculties other than merely those of the five senses. The mind (which is, after all, a mental energy field) is capable of directly receiving imprints of ideas or images through its linkage with the high-frequency energies ruled by Uranus. Thus the subtle planes become a direct source of information or data input. The telepathic relationship with the Universal Mind and other minds make possible a vastly expanded mental awareness. Great inventiveness and originality of thought, sometimes manifesting as genius, go with Mercury-Uranus contacts.

When Mercury is linked with Neptune, the effects are similar to those when Mercury is linked with Uranus in that intuitive powers are manifest. The areas of interest differ in that the Mercury-Neptune contact leads more toward fields that deal with the emotions, such as art, music, drama, poetry, psychology, religion and philosophy.

There is a vivid sense of imagery and highly developed powers of visualization with Mercury-Neptune contacts. For this reason these natives make excellent photographers and cinematographers. The imaginative faculty is highly developed and often used in some manner. There can be an interest in metaphysical studies such as astrology, yoga, and telepathy.

Mercury linked with Pluto extends the powers of the mind into the realms of the microcosm, where matter is seen as crystallized energy and the ultimate basis of reality can be understood. Those advanced souls who have developed this highest faculty of the mind are apt to work in fields such as atomic physics and occult science. A high degree of clairvoyance linked with the intelligence to understand what is seen characterizes this contact. Such natives may appear inscrutable and mysterious, sometimes having an aura of mystery about them.

For some these contacts will not make a major difference in life if the rest of the horoscope does not indicate that the occult planets have sufficient power to be a dominant influence in the native's life. Mercury-Pluto aspects must be reinforced by other aspects in order to bring out their full potential.

Mercury linked with the Moon indicates that the native is occupied with the mundane, practical affairs of life. Matters of food, housing, clothing, and physical comforts in general are apt to occupy much of the native's attention.

The native will be practical about everyday matters and will manage these affairs in an efficient way. However, the native may bore others with his constant chatter about personal matters and inconsequential things.

When Mercury is linked with the Sun, there is much will-power connected with the mind. This is good if the native is motivated to greater accomplishment and higher achievement through the use of the mind. There is, however, danger of an egocentric view of the world, and the native may lack objectivity about self, often being unwilling to face facts impartially when self-esteem and the esteem of others is at stake.

The power of the Sun can illuminate Mercury and give it a penetrating vision and understanding. People with the Sun conjunction Mercury can inspire others with their mental leadership. They possess a great deal of creative ability in the use of their minds. This comes from the strength of concentration that the power principle of the Sun gives to Mercury.

Mercury in the Air Element

Mercury functions at its best in the air triplicity. This is because the air signs, being signs of association and relationship, give the mind a more universal awareness that leads to impartiality and an objective, impersonal vision of the truth. The reason for this is readily apparent: Mercury rules Gemini, the sign of ideas, travel, communication, writing, and speech. The Gemini-Mercury person is quick, agile, alert, and a seeker of knowledge.

In Libra, Mercury is given an awareness of the "not-self" or of other people and is thus given a more well-rounded and multi-faceted view of reality. This comes from the influence of Venus, which gives friendliness and consideration of others, making possible an open and rapid communication with them.

Saturn's exaltation in Libra gives the Libra Mercury a strong sense of justice and discipline and a capacity for organized study, work, and learning. Out of this sense of orderly procedure and graceful expression the impartial truth emerges in balance with due consideration of all available facts and experience.

People with Mercury in Libra are moderate and do not like excess and extremes in their decisions. Such people are aware that happiness depends upon the mutual balance and cooperation of all the necessary processes of life. Their concern is to maintain this balance and to build upon it in an organized and orderly way. This is particularly true of the middle decan of Libra (Aquarius decan) with a sub-rulership of Saturn and Uranus. This adds discipline and intuitive linkage with the super-conscious mind to the faculties of the everyday, practical mind. The third decan of Libra is also a good position of Mercury because of its Gemini sub-rulership, which strengthens the thinking ability, speed and agility of the mind.

Mercury in the first decan of Libra is more concerned with people and social relationships; they are people-oriented rather than principle-oriented, as compared to the other decans. If not highly developed, they can be flighty and superficial, merely concerned with getting the attention of others rather than accomplishing something important and worthwhile.

Mercury in the first decan of Gemini has a double Mercury influence. This Mercury represents intelligence and reasoning ability in its most pure form. Because of its extreme neutrality, it is one of the most unstable positions; the native has a tendency to flit from one subject to another without sufficiently sustained concentration to master one field well enough for it to be of practical value.

Mercury in the middle decan of Gemini, which has a Libra, Venus, and Saturn sub-influence, is inclined to be more occupied with social thoughts and artistic expression. This Mercury position acquires some of the Libra attributes of weighing and balancing and a strong sense of justice. The native is apt to be circumspect and judicious in thought and communication.

The third decan of Gemini is one of the most powerful positions of Mercury. Mercury here retains all its quick Gemini reasoning ability and in addition acquires steadiness of concentration and superconscious intuitive ability that arises from the Saturn-Uranus rulership of Aquarius. This Aquarius sub-rulership also gives a double Mercury impetus because Mercury is exalted in Aquarius. The mind is at once able to function on and communicate between two levels of consciousness, the practical reasoning level, and the superconscious level of direct intuitive experience. The mind is able to tune in and interpret from the Universal Mind and give this knowledge practical application.

Mercury in Aquarius is in the sign of its greatest power, or sign of exaltation. Here the practical mind has the direct resources of the superconscious Universal Mind, which can transcend the limitations of the personal ego.

The individual mind is but a lower overtone reflection of the high-frequency energy field (ruled by Uranus) which is the Universal Mind. Through a process of reflecting on a lower overtone, Mercury in Aquarius is able to give concrete expression to ideas and thoughts found in this realm of subtle energy, the Universal Mind.

It is through the principle of Saturn, which stabilizes the mental field, making it like a polished mirror, that the intuitive powers of Uranus focused through the mind are able to manifest. This is to say that Mercury cannot reach Uranus without the organizing power of Saturn, which is needed to steady the attention, making the mind coherent enough to tune in to the higher Uranian levels of consciousness.

Mercury in the first decan of Aquarius has a sub-influence of Saturn and Uranus such that mental intuition is highly developed and all that applies to Mercury's exaltation in Aquarius applies to this first decan most strongly.

Mercury in the second decan of Aquarius has a Gemini sub-influence with a double Mercury connotation. Therefore, this

Mercury is more intellectual and practical in its mental application than Mercury in the other two decans. It uses the Aquarius intuition but is concerned with applying it to practical mental affairs. These natives are more concerned with the usefulness of their ideas; originality is secondary.

Mercury in the third decan of Aquarius has a sub-influence of Venus and Saturn. Here the resources of the mind are disciplined by Saturn and inspired by Uranus but find expression in social and artistic endeavors. This native is friendly and socially inclined, interested in learning what other people think and the way in which they express themselves. These people make good psychologists and social workers. They are to be humanitarian in a just and personal, yet objective, way.

Mercury in the Fire Element

Mercury in Aries gives mental initiative. The native is inspired to use mental energy in new ways to achieve a desired goal. These natives have the ability to be intensely aware of the here-and-now of the situation, thus enabling them to take advantage of all new opportunities as they present themselves.

The danger of Mercury in Aries is that of seeing life only from one's own point of reference. If carried too far, this can lead to argumentation and mental conceit. The way to avoid these pitfalls is to assume the objective, impersonal attitude of an observer. Mercury in Aries gives dauntless mental courage to keep trying to find new solutions to problems. If this ability can be coupled with both follow-through the steadiness of purpose, much can be accomplished.

Mercury in the first decan of Aries has a double Mars connotation that gives dynamic will to the mental process, providing it does not become mental arrogance. These natives will fight for any cause or idea with which they identify themselves.

Mercury in the second decan of Aries has a Sun connotation. This position confers willpower and creative ability. These natives have the ability to gather around themselves those who will carry out the ideas they initiate. There is a fixity of purpose to the basic Mars active desire-action principle affecting the mind. This is coupled with inspiration and creativity, which adds a steadying influence to the pure Mars action force.

Mercury in the third decan of Aries has a Jupiter connotation, an influence that gives a degree of spiritual insight, good will, benevolence, and the optimism that gives power to positive thinking. These philosophical Jupiter overtones can have a guiding and a balancing effect on the aggressive Mars energy affecting this Mercury position. These natives are apt to have a developed sense of fair play and honor where mental interaction with the world is concerned.

Often there is a prophetic insight that guides the mental processes of the native when embarking on a new course of action. There is vision of new opportunities of growth and expansion that is not apparent to others.

Mercury in the Sun-ruled sign of Leo gives the mind broad and penetrating powers of insight because the mind is illumined by the light of the Sun. This position of Mercury gives the native the ability to back up decisions with willpower. Because they express their ideas with clarity, they are able to influence the thinking of others and often mold public opinion. They have the power to express the mind in an inspirational and creative way; therefore they generate enthusiasm for ideas in others, gaining their support. They are also skillful in the teaching of children, so they make good educators.

Mercury in the first decan of Leo has a double Sun impetus. For this reason these natives are apt to be strongly independent and self-willed in their opinions. Mercury in Leo possesses a great deal of mental creative power. Here we have a mind that can be dictatorial because of its tendencies to identify the ego with certain favorite ideas. If this is overcome, however, these natives can be powerful forces for good because of their big and powerful ideas that can promote and espouse noble causes.

Mercury in the second decan of Leo has a Jupiter influence. This increases altruism and social awareness, giving prophetic insight to the native's capacity for leadership and progressive ideas. Their sense of justice, fair play, and altruism wins the willing cooperation and support of others.

The ideas of these natives benefit the community at large. This decan indicates an interest in the use of philosophy, religion, and education to better human life. A good education contributes to the success of this position.

Mercury in the third decan of Leo has a Mars influence that gives these natives the courage of their convictions.

The managerial ability that Mercury in Leo gives in this decan is combined with decisiveness in acting on new ideas; therefore, these natives are able to adjust quickly and energetically to new circumstances. There is a pioneering spirit and a resourcefulness in crisis situation.

Mercury in Sagittarius is a position that expands and broadens the mind. Those having this position are interested in philosophy, religion, higher education, and travel. Their motives are altruistic and far-sighted. They set goals for themselves and are very one-pointed toward the achievement of those goals. There is a tendency with Mercury in Sagittarius to be dogmatic and make attitudes or pet philosophic dogmas more important than facts.

Mercury is in its detriment in this sign. At times this detriment manifests as impatience with details because the native is only interested in the broader spectrum of life. If this attitude is carried too far, it can lead to impracticality and miscalculation because the success of a project can hinge on one small detail.

Mercury in the first decan of Sagittarius has a double Jupiter influence; therefore, these natives are very optimistic and make good ministers, professors, teachers, and writers. They also make good lawyers. This decan of Sagittarius loves travel and foreign places. They can be spiritually inspired and their ideas can awaken faith and optimism in others.

Mercury in the second decan of Sagittarius has a Mars influence. These natives are true adventurers; they like to propel themselves into circumstances and situations that will increase their knowledge and experience. For this reason they often have an interest in sports and make good sports announcers, writers, and reporters. They have a dauntless optimism and they will not take no for an answer.

Mercury in the third decan of Sagittarius has a Sun influence that gives leadership ability, willpower, and steadiness of purpose to the expression of the native's social, religious, and educational ideas. This position often makes one a leader in the realms of creative thought that deal with law, religion, philosophy, and education. There is a mental strength with this position that inspires confidence in their leadership.

Mercury in the Earth Element

Mercury in Taurus gives a slow, steady, practical mind. These natives are slow to make decisions, and once made do not like to change them. If Mercury in Taurus is expressed in a negative way, they can be stubborn and opinionated. However, they are thorough in making and carrying out plans. This position is not necessarily conducive to originality of thought; however, there is a good deal of common sense and skill in thinking connected with moneymaking, business planning, and economic matters.

Mercury in Taurus makes one slow and deliberate in speech. There is also a mental appreciation of beauty, art, symmetry, and proportion. Because of the practical and methodical nature of this position, there is often a great deal of mathematical ability.

Mercury in the first decan of Taurus has a double Venus connotation. These people are often knowledgeable about farming and methods of food production. There is also a mental appreciation of structural beauty, art, and symmetry. This position of Mercury is good for financial planning and business people.

Mercury in the second decan of Taurus has a Virgo-Mercury connotation. This is one of the best positions of Mercury for practical, detailed thinking. These natives have the ability to plan their work in the most efficient way possible. They make excellent builders and craftspeople because they understand the use of tools. They also possess the necessary patience to learn useful crafts and skills.

Mercury in the third decan of Taurus has a Saturn influence. Thus these natives are apt to be ambitious, using their minds to attain material success. Because of the mental discipline inherent in the Saturn influence of this position, they make good designers, architects, and mathematicians. These natives are apt to judge the merit of any idea on the basis of its practical usefulness.

Mercury in Virgo is in the sign of its rulership and therefore it is in one of the better positions, especially where exactness in detail and practicality of thought are required. By comparison, Mercury in Virgo possesses more exactness, more discipline in detail, and more mental patience and precision than does a Mercury in Gemini. The Mercury-Gemini native is apt to express more originality of thought. For the preceding reasons Mercury in Virgo is excellent for researchers, accountants, mathematicians and statisticians, physicians, and any profession requiring skill and precision.

Mercury in Virgo can be counted on to analyze any situation and figure out the most efficient way of getting a job done. The tendency of Mercury in Virgo is to analyze or break down the subject of study or work into its component parts, thus gaining an understanding of how the parts are related to make the whole.

If expressed in a negative way, this position of Mercury can seem picayune and overly critical. These qualities can at times exasperate others. However, the success of an enterprise may hinge on the smallest detail, and an awareness of such details is where Mercury in Virgo shines. People with this position of Mercury are interested in and concerned about diet, cleanliness, neatness, and good hygiene.

Mercury in the first decan of Virgo has a double Mercury influence. These natives make excellent scholars and researchers and will have immense patience in getting to the bottom of any matter at which they work or study. They make good librarians and efficiency experts, being skillful in their work because they understand all the details that are involved in the job they are doing. They often come up with ideas for expediting work more efficiently. These natives make interesting and lucid writers on scientific subjects, and there is often a keen interest in science and mathematics.

Mercury in the second decan of Virgo has a Saturn influence. This position gives a highly-disciplined, organized, and hard-working mental attitude. These natives often make good designers, builders, architects, engineers, and mathematicians.

Any work requiring extreme precision, such as optics or machining, appeals to them. If expressed in a negative way, this position can lead to critical attitudes and pessimism. This position confers exactitude of thought and the structure-building aspect of the mind is highly developed. These natives seek education in order to further their career ambitions.

Mercury in the third decan of Virgo has a Venus-Taurus influence. These natives are apt to be interested in the detailed tasks and thinking concerned with their work or business and also in business planning. They can be skillful in banking, accounting, and financial management. There can be a scholarly interest in art and its history, and there is usually a high degree of mental patience and perseverance.

Mercury in Capricorn indicates a mind that is highly organized, disciplined, ambitious, and practical. These natives seek education for purposes of career, ambition, and the financial success it confers. They make good executive planners of business enterprises and skillful and efficient managers. With this position of Mercury, everything is appraised for its practical value. These natives often have mathematical ability and a planning capacity that helps them achieve their objective. They are conservative in their thinking and do not like to take unnecessary risks or gambles. They mentally identify with established institutions and conservative political thought.

Mercury in the first decan of Capricorn has a double Saturn influence. These natives have a great deal of mental discipline. However, they are apt to be conservative and traditional in their thinking. Expressed in a positive way, their thoughts can have a crystal clarity because of their good organization. Expressed in a negative way they are apt to be pessimistic and tradition-bound. They make decisions slowly and carefully and do not change them easily. There is the ability to study and to learn from past experience.

Mercury in the second decan of Capricorn has a Venus-Taurus influence. These natives are as a rule well-organized and enterprising in their thinking about business and financial matters and because of this they make good financial planners, executives, statisticians, and accountants. There also can be an interest in architecture as a practical art form.

Mercury in the third decan of Capricorn has a Mercury-Virgo influence. This position of Mercury makes one very practical and skillful in thought concerning work and detail. The natives can be of help to the individual worker as he or she performs a task through providing direction, teaching, and supervision. These people are at their best when working with an individual rather than with a group. These natives are highly efficient and organized, often possessing considerable mathematical and research ability.

If expressed in a negative way, these people can be critical, fault-finding, and pessimistic. They make good troubleshooters in any business or enterprise where a process or a product needs to have the bugs ironed out.

Mercury in the Water Element

Mercury in Cancer is not one of the best positions for this planet because the native's mind is subject to emotional prejudices based on past conditioning and are generally the result of family breeding and heredity patterns. These natives are apt to talk incessantly about trivial domestic matters that are of no concern to those around them.

They tend to arrive at decisions intuitively rather than logically. This intuitive mind is not always of the highest quality since emotional prejudices in the native's unconscious can influence the thinking. There is also a mental inertia, making the natives cling to traditional family ideas and attitudes that represent emotional security to them.

However, Mercury in this sign can give a good memory, sympathy as well as empathy, and a practicality about domestic matters. There can also be good business sense in respect to land, housing, and commodities used in the home. There is a tendency to take daily sensory experiences in a very personal way.

Mercury in the first decan of Cancer has a double Moon influence. The thinking of these natives is particularly influenced by their emotional responses. However it does give insight into the emotions and feelings of others. These people may be ultra-sensitive and thin-skinned, making them somewhat touchy; they can imagine slights where none are intended. At the same time they may be overly susceptible to flattery. For them to take praise or blame in an impersonal way is difficult.

These natives are apt to be interested in diet and food. Because Mercury also rules food and because Cancer rules the stomach, there are many excellent cooks and chefs with this decan of Mercury. They may take up occupations involving clothing and water, such as managing laundries.

Mercury in the second decan of Cancer has a Mars-Pluto connotation. These natives possess a little more willpower and aggressiveness than do those with Mercury in either of the other two decans of Cancer. They are capable of being vindictive and scornful in speech if they are crossed, but they do possess a penetrating intellect which is able to get to the bottom of things and ferret out mysteries. There is also the ability to analyze experience and to correct past mistakes.

Mercury in the third decan of Cancer has a Neptune influence. The thinking of these natives is highly influenced by psychic and intuitive faculties. They are able to tune into the universal unconsciousness and draw from it the information they need.

People with this position of Mercury are often psychics and clairvoyants. They have a tendency to absorb information by osmosis rather than through disciplined study; therefore, they often possess knowledge about things without knowing why they do possess it.

Mercury in Scorpio can give a shrewd and penetrating mind that is capable of comprehending life's inner secrets and subtle forces. This ability may manifest itself through a knowledge of the occult or sciences such as medicine, chemistry, and physics. Such natives also make good investigators and detectives. The Sherlock Holmes archetype fits Mercury in Scorpio. These natives are apt to be secretive and to speak only when it serves a definite purpose. In this way they create an air of mystery about themselves, thus giving them the listening ear of others when they do speak. Their speech is forceful and dramatic when it is employed.

These natives are keen observers and there is little that escapes their penetrating gaze. In some cases there can be argumentativeness and vindictiveness that leads to sharp comments and stinging, barbed remarks. They make first-class critics and debunkers and their judgment is accurate although not always charitable. They generally perceive the truth of what is really happening.

Mercury in the first decan of Scorpio has a double Mars-Pluto influence. In addition, because of Uranus' exaltation in Scorpio, there can be an ability to make fast intuitive decisions in times of crises. These natives mince no words and have no tolerance for nonsense and wishy-washy attitudes. There is a tendency to take extreme partisan viewpoints that make them strong propagandists and vehement debaters.

In the case of highly-developed individuals there is a profound insight into the internal and subtle forces that govern the universe. These natives are extremely resourceful, possessing mental endurance and skill that help them to overcome obstacles that would crush others who are less endowed.

Mercury in the second decan of Scorpio has a Neptune-Jupiter influence. These natives tend to be somewhat more religious and mystical in their thinking. They too are highly intuitive and are sometimes clairvoyant. This decan position of Mercury has a greater degree of emotional empathy and understanding than does Mercury in the first decan of Scorpio. This is because the exaltation sign of Venus is Pisces and is therefore included in the influences on the Pisces decan of Mercury in Scorpio. The Jupiter influence makes these natives concerned about social reform and well-being, while the Neptune influence tends to make them mystical in their mental outlook. When this is combined with the Pluto-Uranus influence of Scorpio there is a highly occult mental outlook, making this position sensitive to subtle psychic impressions.

Mercury in the third decan of Scorpio has a Moon influence. For this reason the thinking of these natives is strongly influenced by their emotional reactions and emotional memories. They have vivid powers of recall and good memory; however, they should be careful not to allow past misfortunes and slights to bias their thinking. There is a tendency for strong emotional reactions that can lead to verbal sarcasm and bitterness.

They are strongly committed to help their family, working in practical ways to further those to whom they are related by family ties.

Mercury in Pisces gives a mind that is intuitive and perceptive in a very subtle way. They are not logical thinkers; instead they have a keen perception and sensitivity to the psychic forces at work in their environment and relationships. They can learn more through a natural psychic awareness than they do through speech or study. Much of the learning process goes on in the unconscious mind and later filters up to the conscious awareness when it is needed. Often these people are considered to be visionaries and dreamers. However, they make excellent poets, artists, and fiction writers because of their sensitive imagination. This artistic ability arises out of their internal visualization or image-making capacities. They have an ability to see things complete in all details as though they were watching an internal movie projection screen. Thus their perceptions of reality can have depth and vividness. They are also sympathetic and kind-hearted when it comes to understanding the problems of others. Because they possess much psychological insight and a sort of telepathic rapport with other people, they can make good psychologists and spiritual teachers and advisors.

If Mercury is afflicted in this sign, there is danger of mental chaos and confusion. The thinking mind is at the mercy of all kinds of unconscious psychological neuroses and aberrations based on past emotional conditioning that can distort the present time perception of reality. This is a very sensitive Mercury, and these people should be taught early in life how to direct their attention and thus control their thoughts through meditation and work. However, as a rule these people do not respond well to rigid disciplines that prevent a natural intuitive response to life.

Mercury in the first decan of Pisces has a double Neptune connotation. These natives are mystical thinkers who have a deep connection with their own unconscious mind. Because of this they can tap universal levels of spiritual awareness that span all levels of human history and experience. There is thus the possibility of great spiritual wisdom and an understanding that can be used to uplift and help others. Sometimes this manifests through work as a clairvoyant channel or medium to bring forth deeper levels of spiritual knowledge and prophetic vision. However, there is also danger of mental lassitude, lack of direction, and a tendency to drift without purpose through daydreaming or dislike of disciplined mental tasks. These natives can possess a vivid imagination and good powers of visualization often manifest as the ability to see final results of future events and conditions in their mind's eye. There is often a keen appreciation of music, poetry, literature, and art.

Mercury in the second decan of Pisces has a Moon influence. Here we have a very personal Mercury where the thinking is strongly colored by the personal emotional reactions that affect thinking through the unconscious mind. These natives are apt to have strong likes and dislikes where other people are concerned. This liking takes on a peculiar nature, which seems to exist for no obviously apparent reason, and at times is irrelevant as to the worth of the person on whom it is bestowed.

Such natives can have a deep attachment to their home and family that occupies much of their mental thought and effort. Their thinking is deeply colored by unconscious influences stemming from early childhood conditioning.

The third decan of Pisces is perhaps the most spiritually profound decan of the zodiac. This is because of the sub-influence of Uranus and Pluto, which are the higher octaves and exalted rulers of Scorpio and thus of this third Scorpio decan of Pisces. The subtle influence of all three of the outer occult planets, plus the energy of Mars, are brought to bear in this decan.

It is a spiritual summing up of the entire experience of all the signs of the zodiac. Thus in highly developed persons Mercury in this decan can be vast and penetrating in spiritual understanding and discernment expressed through the mind. A real spiritual transformation of the mind takes place in this decan in preparation for a new beginning in Aries. The Mars sub-influence gives this process energy and courage and sharpness.

If this third decan of Pisces is afflicted there can be danger of mental exhaustion, lack of focus and influences that can interfere with the native's proper unfoldment. These natives can be excellent writers on occult subjects. When properly used, Mercury in this decan of Pisces has unlimited potentialities for expansion into cosmic levels of awareness.

Retrograde Mercury

Mercury rules communication, and except for the Moon, it is the fastest moving planet.

Therefore, the effects of Mercury when it is stationary or retrograde are even more noticeable than the effects of retrograde motion of other planets.

The times when Mercury is retrograde are apt to be times of delays of information, confusion, and indecisiveness, which often results from the breakdown of normal channels of communication.

Actually there is no such thing as a planet moving backward in its orbit. Rather, the planets sometimes appear to move backward as seen from Earth because of one planet overtaking the other in its revolution around the Sun.

It is generally not a good idea to make important decisions when Mercury is retrograde because they are apt to be delayed, changed, or not carried out as originally planned. Often it is not possible to make a conclusive decision or finish a matter until Mercury goes direct again. Mercury retrograde indicates a time of mental backtracking when decisions and ideas are revised and reexamined.

A horoscope in which Mercury is retrograde at birth can indicate a person who is forced by life to re-learn old lessons and thoroughly reevaluate his or her thinking. In other words, Mercury retrograde in a natal chart makes for more introspection and a slower pace of expressed ideas in communication.

The year when by progression Mercury turns direct or retrograde indicates a major mental turning point in a person's life, involving the houses that Mercury rules and occupies and the sign that Mercury occupies as well as the affairs ruled by the planets that aspect Mercury.

When Mercury turns direct, by progression, a person becomes more outwardly expressive mentally and his thought and learning ability is speeded up. When Mercury turns retrograde by progression, a person is apt to become more secretive, introspective and withdrawn from communication with the outside world.

If Mercury is retrograde in a *fixed* sign, it is hard to get needed information and decision-making becomes weighty and indecisive. If the retrograde motion occurs in a *mutable* sign, there can be confusion, vacillation, and indecision. If the retrograde motion occurs in a *cardinal* sign, there can be false starts and much rushing about without well-considered planning and organization.

Mercury in the Houses

Mercury in the First House: Mercury in the first house indicates a person with a mental outlook on life. These natives are quick-witted and changeable in their mannerisms. They are highly communicative and are apt to talk a great deal. Speech and writing are their primary means of self-expression. Their actions are based on that which seems logically to make the most sense to them; therefore, they are not apt to project themselves in any way that is contrary to their reasoning. These people can be appealed to through the use of logic and reasoning or through arousing their curiosity. They have a great interest in knowing as much as possible about their environment, giving them a love of knowledge and a striving after education and intellectual attainment.

These natives are apt to be writers, teachers, librarians, secretaries, researchers, scientists, or scholars because they express themselves most readily in these areas. They are apt to think before they act, more so than the average individual.

Mercury in the Second House: Mercury in the second house indicates natives who use their intellect primarily for monetary or material acquisition. These natives make shrewd business people and students of business and economics. They are apt to plan their financial endeavors methodically, especially if Mercury is in an earth sign. They have many ideas for making money, and they also evaluate ideas in terms of their practical value in producing material gain. They acquire knowledge for its practical use rather than for sheer curiosity or scholarly endeavor. They make excellent business planners and economic advisors in large corporate enterprises and are apt to earn money through writing, lecturing, research, teaching, and clerical occupations.

The affairs ruled by the planet that most closely aspects Mercury are also an avenue through which the native can make money.

Mercury in the Third House: Mercury in the third house indicates natives who are especially bright and skillful in all kinds of practical mental work. Since Mercury is in its own house here, these people make excellent writers, lecturers, reporters, and researchers. They are apt to have many original ideas and can solve practical problems, so this position of Mercury is good for inventors and innovators of all types.

There is apt to be active communications with brothers and sisters and with neighbors and coworkers. There can also be much communication in all forms, emailing, telephoning, texting, and short-distance traveling.

The constant flow of new ideas keeps them continually active and in a somewhat agitated state of mind.

Mercury in the Fourth House: Mercury in the fourth house indicates that the mind is quite engaged in family affairs and domestic matters. The home conditions are subject to much activity and to frequent change of residence.

These natives are apt to use the home as a place of intellectual activity. Often they collect a large library and conduct discussions and sometimes learning activities or study groups in the home.

Mercury in this house can indicate that the native's work is centered in the house or that they work from the home. The house is used in some ways as a communication center with many messages received and sent from it. One or both of the parents may be highly educated or engaged in an intellectual occupation. These natives are apt to place a lot of importance on the acquiring of knowledge as part of the family life.

Mercury in the Fifth House: Mercury in the fifth house indicates that the natives enjoy intellectual games and pastimes. Their pleasures are apt to be of an intellectual sort such that they enjoy mental rather than physical pleasures. There is also an interest in the education of children so that these natives make excellent elementary and middle school teachers.

These natives understand and are apt to be successful in occupations dealing with pleasures, amusements, entertainment, and courtship. Their keen creative imagination also gives them ability as actors, poets, and playwrights.

Mercury in the Sixth House: Mercury in the sixth house indicates people who are extremely good at accurate, detailed work that requires careful study, concentration, and efficient use of work methods and techniques. This arises out of the native's mental ambition to accomplish something notable and praiseworthy. They are neat and well-organized in their work methods, as well as their thinking processes.

They can easily be irritated by people who do not have the same standards of neatness and order in their work environment. Their mastery of order and technique makes them so efficient that they often accomplish twice as much in the same amount of time as others do when doing the same kind of work.

There is often an interest in diet, health, or hygiene. They make excellent physicians, nurses, medical personnel, and dieticians, or they may travel for reasons of health or work.

Mercury in the Seventh House: Mercury in the seventh house indicates natives who are both interested and curious about what other people think. They are especially concerned about good communication with the partner or spouse or with the public at large. This may lead to a mental interest in matters of justice and a study of the law.

This position of Mercury is good for people engaged in selling, public speaking, or public relations. They have a natural ability to see the other person's point of view and to perceive whether others understand what the native is trying to say to them. These natives also do well in the study of psychology, sociology, and social relations.

These natives are apt to marry someone who is younger or who is an employee. They can be related in some manner or the marriage partner could be mentally inclined, well-educated, or idea oriented.

Mercury in the Eighth House: Mercury in the eighth house indicates people who are interested in corporate finance, taxes, death or the affairs of the dead, and scientific or occult mysteries.

There is also the ability to make money through Mercurial occupations carried on in partnership with another person. Often these people remain mentally conscious until the very moment of death.

They are interested in reading and are sometimes authors of mystery novels or suspense stories. There is a mental fascination with all kinds of hidden mysteries that can be expressed as an interest in the deeper aspects of science, the occult, and life after death.

These natives have the ability to ferret out secrets and get to the bottom of things. They are strongly affected by the death of a brother, sister, or neighbor, which can cause them much mental anguish. There may be journeys because of deaths.

With Mercury in this position, one often finds those who are interested in communicating with the dead.

Mercury in the Ninth House: Mercury in the ninth house indicates natives who are interested in higher education, law, philosophy, and religion. They will seek a university education if at all possible, often going on to advanced aspects of study involving postgraduate work.

They often work as professors, lawyers, foreign correspondents, authors, publishers, or ministers. Even in the horoscope of the ordinary person, there will be an interest in philosophy, religion, and man's ultimate purpose in the universe. These natives are fond of travel and often visit and study in foreign countries. They have a great curiosity about history, other cultures and faraway places.

These natives often expand ideas and philosophical outlooks as their minds become illumined by higher thought and intuitive knowledge.

Mercury in the Tenth House: Mercury in the tenth house indicates people who are apt to seek education as a means to career advancement and achievement of some form of fame and renown.

These natives want to be respected and admired for their knowledge and intellectual achievements. Having an advanced or professional degree means a great deal to them because of the respect and status it confers. Often the native's profession is of a mental sort, such as being a writer, professor, reporter, scientist, or researcher. Their success depends upon the amount of education they receive, so they generally get as much education as they can.

Often these natives attain success through holding an important, responsible position working in a large organization. They can achieve fame through making a unique contribution in a field of human knowledge. The planet that most closely aspects Mercury can also be an indicator of the profession.

Mercury in the Eleventh House: Mercury in the eleventh house indicates natives who are mentally occupied with humanitarian ideals and group activities.

There is a tendency to get involved in many intellectual friendships with people who are mentally oriented, such as writers, scientists, teachers, and students. This position of Mercury can indicate many acquaintances but few lasting friends. These natives seek associations with people who can increase their knowledge and help them acquire a better job or position.

With this position of Mercury we have people who are mentally concerned about humanitarian pursuits and causes. These natives should be especially careful about signing papers or making a financial commitment for a friends. There can also be the tendency to be analytical and therefore critical of friends.

Mercury in the Twelfth House: Mercury in the twelfth house indicates people who are shy or secretive about expressing their thoughts and ideas. Often there is a deep insight into the workings of the unconscious mind that can give an interest in psychology or occult studies or the ability to gain ideas through telepathic sources.

The mind is capable of carrying on thinking processes on the unconscious level, such that these natives get an intuitive flash that brings a solution to conscious awareness as result of the unconscious reasoning process arriving at a solution. Natives with this position of Mercury often go to bed with a problem on their mind and wake up with a solution.

Sometimes this position indicates that the natives are mentally prey to unconscious neuroses and confusing psychic influences, especially if Mercury is afflicted.

Should Mercury be in a water sign in the twelfth house, the native learns more by osmosis than by well-ordered study procedures. There is also a tendency for the native to be unconsciously mentally influenced through subliminal sensory impressions.

The Importance of Mercury in the Horoscope

CHAPTER TWO

The Minor Aspects

M inor aspects are an important but often overlooked part of astrological analysis. In some cases, a minor aspect of exact orb can be more significant than a major aspect of wide orb.

When considering planets in the natal horoscope that lack close major aspects, it is especially important to determine whether these same planets have minor aspects that are significant.

Another important factor to consider with the minor, as well as the major, aspects is the approaching or departing nature of the aspect. This concept is *not* to be confused with applying and separating aspects; instead, it deals with the synodical cycle of the planets involved in the aspect. If the faster-moving planet is moving away from the conjunction to the slower-moving planet—that is, the conjunction has already been formed and the opposition has yet to take place—it is said to be departing. If the Sun and Moon were making a departing aspect, the Moon would be waxing; in other words, it's the time between the New Moon and the Full Moon, which has yet to occur.

If the aspect is an approaching one, the faster-moving planet is moving away from the opposition to the slower-moving planet toward the conjunction to it. If the Sun and Moon are involved in an approaching aspect, this would occur during the waning phases of the Moon. The waning phases of the Moon occur when the Full Moon has already occurred and the New Moon has yet to occur.

Whether the minor aspects are approaching or departing makes a considerable difference when accounting for the sign, decanate, and duad to which the aspect corresponds in the natural zodiac. Also, the planetary rulers of the signs, decanates, and duads influence the nature of the aspect.

When any aspect, major or minor, is made by a planet or planets that rule that kind of aspect—as indicated by the signs, decanates, and duads corresponding to that aspect in the natural zodiac—then the influence of that planet or planets becomes very pronounced. For example, a departing sextile made by Mercury will indicate intellectual capabilities as indicated by the Gemini sign, decanate, and duad corresponding to the departing sextile in the natural zodiac.

(For quick reference, see the useful definitions section at the end of this chapter.)

Returning to consideration of the minor aspects, let us look at Chart B: the Moon at 1 Taurus 21 in the tenth house is quintile (72 degrees) Venus at 13 Cancer 08 in the twelfth house. Because the Moon is the faster-moving of the two celestial bodies and is moving away from the opposition to Venus and toward the conjunction, this is defined as an approaching quintile aspect. In this example, the Moon-Venus quintile is almost exact (13 minutes).

The Moon would have to be 1 Tarsus 08 to be exactly quintile to Venus. Since the Moon is at 1 Taurus 21, it is past the exact aspect of 72 degrees and therefore forms a separating aspect. The aspect, properly defined, is thus an approaching, separating quintile.

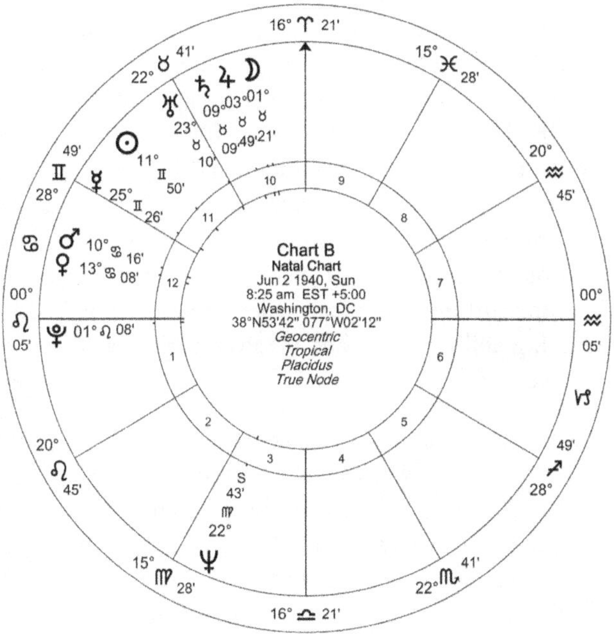
Chart B
Natal Chart
Jun 2 1940, Sun
8:25 am EST +5:00
Washington, DC
38°N53'42" 077°W02'12"
Geocentric
Tropical
Placidus
True Node

The approaching quintile corresponds to the Taurus decanate of Capricorn and the Leo duad of Capricorn. This gives a Saturn-Venus-Moon-Sun-Pluto combination, suggesting good organizational ability, energy, and dynamic self-expression in artistic, social, and business expression. In this case it would indicate practical knowledge and organizational ability in art, beauty, and the creation of artistic expression of various kinds. This quintile is strengthened by the Moon and Venus in mutual reception. Venus is accidentally exalted in the twelfth house, and the Moon is in the sign of its exaltation and dignified by being the most elevated planet in the chart.

The Moon is also the cutting planet of the horoscope, setting the stage for future activities. Because of this strong link between the tenth and twelfth houses, the individual has special talents and abilities for harmoniously linking the intuitive, private, behind-the-scenes activities of his life with his profession and public life. The Moon in the tenth house as the cutting planet and the most elevated one suggests a profession dealing with the public. This would be combined with the intuitive ability to understand the subconscious psychology and motivation of others. The Moon, as ruler of the twelfth house and dispositor of Venus, indicates that this ability could be employed behind the scenes in formulating products that would have mass public appeal. This combination promises financial rewards and public recognition for his activities. The Moon in Taurus in the tenth house as the cutting planet represents the stage being set for further earning ability and public involvement. Such activities often involve women.

The septile (51°25'43") between the Sun at 11 Gemini 50 and Pluto at 01 Leo 08 is the next example of a septile. A wider orb is allowed because the Sun is involved and Pluto is angular and conjunct the Ascendant. The Sun is the faster-moving body and is past the position of the exact septile, so the aspect is separating. Because the Sun is moving away from the opposition, which occurred when the Sun was in Aquarius, and toward the conjunction with Pluto (when the Sun reaches Leo), the aspect is a separating, approaching septile. The approaching septile corresponds to the Aquarius-Saturn-Uranus-Mercury decanate of Aquarius and the Taurus-Venus-Moon duad of Aquarius. Therefore, it partakes of the nature of Saturn, Uranus, Mercury, Venus, and the Moon.

This indicates an ability to harmoniously organize creative projects and unusual ideas, also as indicated by the Sun's position in Gemini in the eleventh house. Because the Sun is in Gemini, ruled by Mercury, and in the eleventh house, corresponding to Aquarius-Uranus-Saturn-Mercury in the natural zodiac and in the Libra decanate and duad of Gemini, thus incorporating the influence of Saturn and Venus, these influences are similar to the planetary influences associated with the approaching septile. Therefore, the intellectual activities, friends, and group associations of the individual constantly influence him to devote effort toward personal self-expression/self-improvement and occult activities, as indicated by Pluto conjunct the natal Leo Ascendant.

Most minor aspects, especially the semi-sextile, septile, and quintile, involve Saturn or Venus or both. These are aspects of cooperation. They confer the ability to deal with the public and also to synthesize diverse activities in a harmonious manner.

For further practice in delineation, study the following minor aspects in the example chart:

- Mercury decile (36°) Pluto

- Mars quintile (72°) Neptune

- Moon nonagon (40°) Sun

- Saturn semi-sextile (30°) Sun

- Sun semi-sextile (30°) Mars

- Sun semi-sextile (30°) Venus

- Pluto septile (51°25'43") Neptune

- Saturn sesquiquadrate (135°) Neptune

- Mars semi-square (45°) Uranus

Only by working with these minor aspects can one understand the full potential of Chart B.

Three Families of Aspects

Minor aspects are grouped into three basic families. The first of these families includes the vigintile (18°), decile (36°), quintile (72°), tri-vigintile (54°) (although the tri-vigintile is not usually listed as an aspect), tridecile (108°), biquintile (144°). These are all based on the division of a circle by 5, 10, and 20, thus forming a harmonic series. This set of aspects is related to the occult and the use of the will, and these angles are found in the pentagram, or five-pointed star, which has a deep occult significance.

This family of aspects relates to the higher synthesis of the four basic elements—fire, earth, air, and water—into the fifth element of Ether; therefore, this family of aspects relates to the use of the spiritual will and transcends physical limitations. These same angles are found in the inner connections of the vertices of the icosahedron and the pentagonal dodecahedron. These structures interrelate tetrahedrons, octahedrons and cubes in a more complex, but ordered, synthesis. The angles of the major aspects are also found in the tetrahedron, octahedron, and cube.

The pentagram or five-pointed star bisects its own lines according to the Golden Mean ratio that is found throughout all nature. Individuals having this first family of aspects in their charts have the opportunity to work with energies that transcend the physical level of manifestation. One of the abilities unique to this family of aspects is the capacity to understand the inner relation between seemingly isolated sets of circumstances.

The next family of minor aspects is the nonagon (40°), bi-nonagon (80°), (trine (120°) is included in this family), and the quad-nonagon (160°). Of all of these aspects, the nonagon and trine are most commonly used. The nonagon is considered a harmonizing influence. The division of the zodiac by three gives 120°, which is the important major aspect called the trine. The nonagon is a third harmonic of the trine and has a similar quality to the trine, although of a more subtle and higher harmonic.

Because of this higher harmonic relation to the trine, it could act as a harmonic link between subtle spiritual dimensions and the ordinary realms of human awareness and activity.

The next family of minor aspects incorporates the semisquare of 45° and the sesquiquadrate of 135°. These two minor aspects belong to a series of aspects that includes the major aspects— the square and the opposition. The opposition is one-half of the circle, the square is one-fourth of the circle, the semi-square is one-eighth of the circle, and the sesquiquadrate is three-eighths of the circle. All of these aspects are divisions of a circle by multiples of two. They bring dramatic occurrences into life that demand immediate attention, work, and practical action, especially if found in cardinal signs. The semi-square and sesquiquadrate aspects often bring irritation and frustration in actions and fulfillment of desires.

Another family of minor aspects involves the semi-sextile and inconjunct, or quincunx. The semi-sextile is an aspect of 30°, or one-twelfth of a circle; the inconjunct is five-twelfths of a circle, or 150°. These aspects are important minor aspects, and could be considered minor major aspects because they relate directly to the twelve-fold pattern of the zodiac, as do all the major aspects that are multiples of the 30° intervals of the signs. The semi-square and sesquiquadrate, if exact, are also important minor major aspects.

The next family is the septile of 51°25'43", the bi-septile of 102°51'26", and the tri-septile of 154°17'08". The septile is one-seventh of a circle and is representative of occult and mystical forces at work in the life of the individual. It operates in subtle, repetitive ways. The bi-septile has a similar quality because it belongs to the same harmonic pattern. The tri-septile indicates subtle intuitive abilities and circumstances in life that have on-going ramifications.

There is also a family of minor aspects based on the division of a circle by elevenths. Eleven is a highly occult number, suggesting that this family of aspects has a quality similar to the septile family, indicating unconscious intuitive forces at work that guide the individual's destiny.

Vigintile

When considering the vigintile aspect of 18°, count 18° clockwise and counterclockwise from 0 Aries in the natural zodiac. This brings us to 12 Pisces (approaching) and 18 Aries (departing). Twelve degrees of Pisces, in the case of the approaching vigintile aspect, corresponds to the Cancer decanate and Cancer duad of Pisces. Cancer is ruled by the Moon, and Jupiter and Neptune, which co-rule Pisces, are exalted in Cancer. This would indicate that the approaching vigintile confers the ability to tap hidden intuitive resources. The individual can achieve success by working in the background and relying upon his inner intuitive direction. This intuitive understanding is based on past experience.

When considering the departing vigintile, 18 Aries, which corresponds to the Leo decanate and the Scorpio duad of Aries, we have the Sun exalted in Aries and ruler of Leo. Mars, as the ruler of Aries and the Scorpio duad, plus Pluto, co-ruler of Aries and exalted in the Leo decanate and co-ruler of the Scorpio duad, give a highly dynamic transformative combination wherein the individual can expand his influence and effectiveness through the application of his will in action. This aspect should be kept within a half degree of orb or less to be effective.

Semi-sextile

When considering the semi-sextile, an aspect of 30°, count thirty degrees from 0 Aries in the natural zodiac both clockwise and counterclockwise; this brings us to 0 Pisces and 0 Taurus.

The departing, second house-Venus-Moon-Taurus kind of semi-sextile gives an ability to accumulate the resources necessary to make steady progress in creative self-expression. It confers a practical sense of how to deal with financial and material conditions in order to achieve security and concrete results. Venus' rulership of Taurus indicates artistic ability of some kind. Since Venus is exalted in Pisces, this is also true of the approaching semi-sextile. The Moon's exaltation in Taurus suggests a mothering, nurturing quality conducive to growth and further expansion. If the semi-sextile has an exact orb, it can be a significant factor in interpretation. Except in the case of hidden aspects, the semi-sextile always links a positive masculine sign with a feminine receptive sign, indicating a harmonizing influence between the masculine and feminine polarities in the individual's expression. The individual is capable of initiating action and dealing with those conditions which he attracts without aggressive effort on his own part. There is an ability to express both of these qualities at the appropriate time and in the appropriate way.

When considering the approaching, twelfth house Neptune-Jupiter-Pisces semi-sextile, the individual has the ability to make use of the refinements of past experience in order to further his present growth and progress. The Neptune-Jupiter influence of Pisces confers the ability to use intuitive faculties and the creative imagination to open the way to further growth. The combination of Venus, Jupiter, and Neptune also confers the qualities of understanding, kindness, and consideration. An orb of three degrees for planets and up to five degrees is allowed if the Sun or Moon is involved in the semi-sextile, The semi-sextile, inconjunct, semi-square, and sesquiquadrate are among the more important minor aspects and therefore a larger orb is allowed.

Decile

When considering the decile aspect, which is one-tenth of a circle or 36°, we count from 0 Aries in a clockwise direction, and this brings us to 24 Aquarius, which belongs to the Libra decanate and the Scorpio duad of Aquarius. Counting in a counter-clockwise direction from 0 Aries brings us to 6 Taurus in the Taurus decanate and Cancer duad of Taurus. Both Taurus and Aquarius are fixed signs, suggesting determination or fixity of purpose in the decile aspect. It would also indicate goal orientation or the ability to work toward a fixed purpose.

When considering the departing Venus-Moon-Jupiter-Neptune-Taurus-Mercury decile, the individual can express qualities of refinement and creative artistic talent. This may be expressed in business, the arts, or in the home environment.

When considering the approaching Aquarius-Uranus-Saturn-Mars-Pluto kind of decile, the individual will express resourcefulness, ingenuity, organization, and scientific understanding. This is a favorable aspect for involvement in the occult or scientific work. It is also a good aspect for work connected with groups and organizations. The division of the circle by 10 suggests the number 1 because 10 reduces to one by adding its digits; 1 is the number associated with willpower, action, and new beginnings. The decile aspect relates to the will or purpose of man's higher spiritual nature and indicates the possibility of the individual being a vehicle for the expression of divine will in some way, as indicated by the planets, signs, and houses involved. This is one of the reasons why this aspect is said to have an occult significance.

Nonagon (Novile)

The nonagon, or nonagile (novile), as it is sometimes called, is one-ninth of a circle or 40°. The departing nonagon corresponds to 10 Taurus in the natural zodiac, belonging to the Virgo decanate and Virgo duad of Taurus. The approaching nonagon corresponds to 20 Aquarius in the Libra decanate and Libra duad of Aquarius. The nonagon has a subtle, mystical, refining quality.

The departing nonagon has a quality related to Venus, the Moon, and Mercury, and it therefore deals with practical knowledge of how to achieve comfort, security, and harmony in the home, the working environment, and financial affairs. It confers faculties of detailed analysis in work methodologies, money management, and creative artistic expression.

The approaching nonagon has qualities related to Uranus, Mercury, Venus, and Saturn. Saturn is particularly important because it co-rules Aquarius and is exalted in the Libra decanate and Libra duad. Therefore, this aspect provides organizational and structural abilities in scientific activities, public relations, working with groups, and legal activities. The nonagon is allowed one degree of orb, or up to two degrees if the Sun or Moon is involved.

Semi-square

The semi-square is an aspect of one-eighth of a circle or 45°. The departing semi-square corresponds to 15 Taurus in the natural zodiac, and the approaching semi-square corresponds to 15 Aquarius in the natural zodiac.

Because Taurus and Aquarius are both fixed signs, irritating and entrenched conditions can be a source of problems for the individual. Because the semi-square belongs to the family of hard-angle aspects, it often brings conditions that demand attention, whether the individual is ready to direct attention to them or not.

The departing semi-square partakes of the nature of Taurus, the Virgo decanate of Taurus, and the Scorpio duad of Taurus. Therefore, it has the qualities of Venus, Moon, Mercury, Mars, Pluto, and Uranus. This type of semi-square can indicate difficulties in financial and business matters that require making decisions that have important long-range consequences. The individual is likely to feel frustrated by financial limitations and difficulties. Intelligent, practical action is required if these difficulties are to be handled properly.

The approaching semi-square partakes of the nature of Aquarius, the Gemini decanate, and the Leo duad. Therefore, it has the nature of Saturn, Uranus, Mercury, Sun, and Pluto. This suggests that an effort of the will is required in order to achieve goals and objectives. Adaptability combined with determination and dedication to a goal is required if progress is to be made. Adaptability is required because sudden and unexpected problems can arise that demand a change of methodology combined with the dedication to the fixed goal. Properly used, the approaching semi-square can be an impetus to intellectual, business, scientific, or professional achievements. Both types of the semi-square can produce frustration, irritation, and dissatisfaction.

The semi-square is allowed an orb of three degrees with planets and up to five degrees if the Sun or Moon is involved.

Septile

The septile is one-seventh of a circle or 51°25'43". The departing septile partakes of the nature of the Capricorn-Saturn-Mars decanate of Taurus and the Capricorn-Saturn-Mars duad of Taurus. Therefore, it has the qualities of Venus, Moon, Saturn, and Mars, indicating skill and organization in the practical implementation of social, artistic, and business goals. Because of the heavy Saturn emphasis, forces of karmic destiny can be at work that guide the individual's course of action to practical fulfillment.

The approaching septile partakes of the nature of the Aquarius-Saturn-Uranus-Mercury decanate of Aquarius and the Taurus-Venus-Moon duad of Aquarius. Here we have the sign of Aquarius and the decanate and duad of Taurus, giving a triple-fixed sign influence. This indicates circumstances and destiny patterns that are guided along a fixed course. Because of the double Saturn influence, karmic forces are at work that guide

The Minor Aspects

the individual according to a predestined pattern. Because of the Uranus and Mercury influences present in this combination, these guiding influences often appear to work through unexpected events and influences.

The septile is allowed an orb of one degree for planets and a degree and a half if the Sun or Moon is involved.

Quintile

The quintile is one-fifth of a circle or 72°. The departing quintile partakes of the nature of the Libra-Venus-Saturn decanate of Gemini and the Libra-Venus-Saturn duad of Gemini. Therefore, it has the qualities of Mercury, Venus, and Saturn. This would indicate detailed, refined organization in the communication and implementation of ideas. It confers grace and skill in diplomacy and public relations. This mutable-cardinal combination confers adaptability combined with ability to act decisively and combine all factors in a harmonious manner. Because of the double Venus influence inherent in this aspect, it is also associated with social and artistic talent.

The approaching quintile corresponds in the natural zodiac to the Virgo-Mercury decanate of Capricorn, and the Virgo-Mercury duad of Capricorn. The approaching quintile has the nature of Saturn, Mars, and Mercury, indicating practical skill in organizing methodologies and implementing ideas. Thus, the individual can be effective in business enterprises and management and skillful in communicating and writing, especially in regard to business. This combination also confers mathematical, engineering, and scientific skills. Both types of quintiles include influences of Saturn, indicating practical and effective skills.

The quintile is given an orb of two degrees for planets and up to three degrees if the Sun or Moon is involved.

Bi-septile

The bi-septile is an aspect of two-seventh of a circle or 102°51'26". The departing bi-septile corresponds to the natural zodiac with the Scorpio-Mars-Pluto-Uranus decanate of Cancer and the Sagittarius-Jupiter-Neptune duad of Cancer. This gives the departing biseptile a Moon, Neptune, Jupiter, Mars, Pluto, and Uranus significance. Jupiter and Neptune are particularly important because they co-rule the Sagittarius duad and are exalted in Cancer. This would suggest the ability to have a transformative influence on existing religious and educational and cultural affairs.

Because Uranus, Neptune, and Pluto are all represented in the combination, the departing bi-septile confers the ability to exercise intuitive abilities and faculties in changing existing educational, cultural, and social conditions. Because Cancer deals with the roots of consciousness, there can be the ability to recover valuable knowledge and information from the past through using the intuition and imagination.

The approaching bi-septile corresponds to the Aries-Mars-Pluto-Sun decanate of Sagittarius and the Gemini-Mercury duad of Sagittarius. This gives the approaching bi-septile a Jupiter, Neptune, Mars, Pluto, Sun, and Mercury combination. This would indicate intuitive guidance and cultural awareness in initiating and implementing ideas relating to educational, cultural, and religious practices and activities. There would be the desire to somehow change and transform existing cultural, educational, religious, and social institutions or lifestyles. This tendency is associated with a curiosity concerning new ideas for cultural lifestyles.

The bi-septile is given only a one degree orb for all planets, including the Sun and Moon.

Tri-decile

The tri-decile is three-tenths of a circle or 108°. The departing tridecile relates to the Scorpio-Mars-Pluto decanate of Cancer and the Pisces-Jupiter-Neptune-Venus duad of Cancer. This combination gives a Moon, Jupiter, Neptune, Mars, Pluto, Uranus, and Venus influence. Jupiter and Neptune are strongly emphasized because of their exaltation in Cancer and their co-rulership of the Pisces duad. When this Jupiter-Neptune influence is combined with the Pluto, Uranus, and Mars influence of the Scorpio decanate, we have an occult, mystical combination, indicating unusual abilities and talents. Much the same as the departing bi-septile, this combination gives intuitive talents for recovering hidden knowledge.

The approaching tri-decile corresponds to the Aries-Mars-Pluto-Sun decanate of Sagittarius and the Aries-Mars-Pluto-Sun duad of Sagittarius. This gives a Jupiter, Neptune, Mars, Pluto, and Sun combination suggesting the desire to be a leader and pioneering of new and better cultural, educational, and religious concepts and lifestyles. There is a tendency to crusade on behalf of personal educational and philosophical beliefs. It is an aspect of optimism, energy, enthusiasm and dynamic expression of the will.

The tridecile is allowed a one degree orb, including the Sun and Moon.

Sesquiquadrate

The sesquiquadrate is an aspect of three eighth of a circle or 135°. The departing sesquiquadrate corresponds to the Sagittarius-Jupiter-Neptune decanate of Leo and the Aquarius-Uranus-Saturn-Mercury duad of Leo. This aspect combines the influences of the Sun, Pluto, Jupiter, Neptune, Saturn, Uranus, and Mercury, giving a range of capabilities. However, this also sug gests a conflict between intellectual and emotional tendencies in creative self-expression. Unexpected limitations, problems, and changes of plan can hinder the individual's freedom of self-expression. The Jupiter-Neptune influence indicates confusion and hidden factors that add to the difficulties in carrying out creative endeavors. This minor aspect indicates a need for greater discipline and personal sensitivity, combined with discernment and organization. Its influence is similar in many respects to the semi-square because it belongs to the same harmonic pattern.

The approaching sesquiquadrate corresponds to the Pisces-Jupiter-Neptune-Venus decanate of Scorpio in the natural zodiac and the Taurus-Venus-Moon duad of Scorpio. It combines the qualities of Mars, Pluto, Uranus, Jupiter, Neptune, Venus, and the Moon. This would suggest a need for clear and realistic handling of financial affairs, as well as anything relating to collective resources. Psychological and sexual difficulties could be an important issue associated with this aspect. Because all three outer planets are represented, proper motivation in the use of occult or psychic abilities becomes a critical issue.

The sesquiquadrate is allowed a three degree orb for planets and up to five degrees if the Sun or Moon is involved.

Bi-quintile

The bi-quintile is an aspect of two-fifths of a circle or 144°. The departing biquintile corresponds to the Aries-Mars-Pluto-Sun decanate of Leo and the Taurus-Venus-Moon duad of Leo. The influences of the Moon, Mars, Pluto, Venus, and the Sun are combined, indicating a dynamic, creative self-expression combined with business, social, and partnership activities. It could also indicate considerable financial activity involving collective resources, along with a practical approach to creative expression.

The approaching biquintile corresponds to the Scorpio-

Mars-Pluto-Uranus decanate of Scorpio and the Capricorn-Saturn-Uranus-Mars duad of Scorpio. Mars, as co-ruler of Scorpio, the Scorpio decanate and exalted ruler of the Capricorn duad, suggests an energetic, innovative, ambitious quality with the approaching biquintile. There is a tendency to want to improve or transform existing conditions. Intensified will power and occult leanings are associated with this aspect.

The biquintile is allowed one degree of orb for planets and up to two degrees if the Sun or Moon is involved.

Inconjunct (Quincunx)

The inconjunct or quincunx is an aspect of five-twelfths of a circle or 150°. The departing inconjunct corresponds to the sign Virgo, the Virgo decanate of Virgo, and the Virgo duad of Virgo. Thus, it is strongly associated with Mercury and the earth element. It demands the proper handling of practical work responsibilities and health consideration through attention to detail, dedication to work, and the intelligent application of practical knowledge.

The approaching inconjunct corresponds in the natural zodiac to the sign Scorpio, Scorpio decanate of Scorpio, and Scorpio duad of Scorpio. It thus has the strong influence of Mars, Pluto, and Uranus.

The approaching inconjunct signifies the need to improve and regenerate existing conditions. It also requires willingness to accept change and detachment from old forms or conditions. It is often associated with death of old conditions and birth of new ones on some level of expression. To achieve this successfully, it is essential to learn the lesson of proper recycling of the waste products of the old as a useful part of the new expression. These waste products can also be mental, emotional, or physical in their nature.

The inconjunct aspect is allowed an orb of three degrees for the planets and five degrees if the Sun or Moon is involved.

Tri-septile

The tri-septile is an aspect of three-sevenths of a circle or 154°17'08".

The departing tri-septile corresponds to the Virgo-Mercury decanate of Virgo and to the Libra duad of Virgo. It has combined qualities of Mercury, Venus, and Saturn. This indicates an intelligent grasp of the requirements necessary to manage public relations, professional affairs, or social activities. It indicates the ability to carry out practical responsibilities in an organized and socially harmonious manner.

The approaching tri-septile corresponds to the Gemini-Mercury decanate of Libra and the Leo-Sun-Pluto duad of Libra. Therefore, it combines the qualities of Venus, Saturn, Mercury, Sun, and Pluto.

This indicates the same practical social abilities indicated by the departing tri-septile, However, it would be combined with qualities of leadership, creative self-expression, and resourcefulness.

The tri-septile is allowed an orb of one degree, even if the Sun or Moon is involved.

Parallel of Declination

The parallel of declination is not an aspect in longitude, as are all other aspects. Parallels are measured in declination, which is the number of degrees and minutes that a planet is north or south of the celestial equator. If two planets are in the same declination, within a degree or less, they are said to be in parallel.

There are two types of parallels: the first occurs when both planets have the same declination within a degree or less and both planets are either north or south of the celestial equator. This kind of planetary configuration is called a parallel and has qualities similar to the conjunction aspect. The other type of parallel is called a contraparallel and occurs when two planets have the same declination within one degree or less, but one is north of the celestial equator and the other is south. This kind of parallel has qualities similar to the opposition aspect.

Both parallels are very dynamic and intense, and give added strength to any other aspects that exist between the two planets that are parallel or contraparallel each other.

In terms of its power or importance, the parallel and contraparallel are considered to be major configurations ranking with the five major aspects. The orb must be kept within one degree in order for it to have the impact of a major aspect.

Definitions

Approaching Aspect: Approaching aspects are formed when the faster-moving planet (or luminary), having contacted the opposition to the slower-moving planet (or luminary), is moving toward the conjunction to that same planet.

Departing Aspect: Departing aspects are formed when the faster-moving planet (or luminary), having contacted the conjunction to the slower-moving planet (or luminary), is moving toward the opposition to that same planet.

Applying Aspect: Applying aspects are formed when the faster-moving planet (or luminary) nears exact aspect to the slower-moving planet (or luminary), moving toward that contact.

Separating Aspect: Separating aspects are formed when the faster-moving planet (or luminary) diverges from exact aspect to the slower-moving planet (or luminary), moving away from that contact.

Semi-sextile: Departing—Taurus-Second House-Venus-Moon—acquiring resources. Approaching—Pisces-Twelfth House-Jupiter-Neptune-Venus—using resources of the subconscious mind and intuition.

Sextile: Departing—Gemini-Third House-Mercury—curiosity, thought, communication. Approaching—Aquarius-Eleventh House-Saturn-Uranus-Mercury—intuitive ideas, friends, and groups.

Square: Departing—Cancer-Fourth House-Moon-Jupiter-Neptune—need to overcome past conditionings and emotional issues. Approaching—Capricorn-Tenth House-Saturn-Mars—hard work to achieve ambitions, need for discipline, structure, and organization.

Trine: Departing—Leo-Fifth House-Sun-Pluto—creative self-expression, enjoyment, personal charisma, vitality. Approaching—Sagittarius-Ninth House-Jupiter-Neptune—inspirational, expansive, intuitive guidance, benefits of religion, philosophy, cultural enrichment, higher education, and travel.

Inconjunct (Quincunx): Departing—Virgo-Sixth House-Mercury—need for efficient and practical approach, hard work, service, efficient methodology, practical thinking. Approaching—Scorpio-Eighth House-Mars-Pluto-Uranus—need to accept the inevitable, changes, transformative death of old attitudes and conditions, need to regenerate motives can bring occult and scientific understanding.

CHAPTER THREE

Interpreting Major and Minor Approaching and Departing Aspects

I t is a gross oversimplification to lump aspects together into general categories of favorable and unfavorable. The basic meaning of each kind of aspect can be derived from the signs and houses of the natural zodiac along with their rulers and exalted rulers. The method for doing this is to count the number of degrees of the aspect in question in a clockwise and counter-clockwise direction from 0 Aries or the first house cusp of the zodiac. Whatever sign and house the number of degrees that completes the aspect is placed in determines the basic interpretive connotation of that kind of aspect.

Let us use the trine as an example. If we go 120° from 0 Aries (or the first house cusp in a timed chart) in a clockwise direction, we arrive at the ninth house cusp and 0 Sagittarius in the natural zodiac. When we go 120° from the first house cusp in a counter-clockwise direction, we arrive at 0 Leo, or the fifth house cusp in a timed chart. The trine aspect has the combined connotation of Leo, the Sun, the fifth house, Sagittarius, Jupiter, Neptune, and the ninth house. Consequently, we can understand why the trine is considered a benefic aspect when it is associated with the life-giving vitality of the Sun, the pleasure orientation of the fifth house, and the creative self-expression of Leo. Associated with the Sagittarius ninth house half of the trine is the expansive, benefic influence of Jupiter and the philosophical and spiritual orientation of Sagittarius and the creative intuitive faculties of Neptune.

Significance of Applying and Separating Aspects

An applying aspect occurs when the faster moving planet is closing in on the exact orb that completes the aspect with the slower moving planet.

A separating aspect occurs when the faster moving planet is moving away from the exact orb that has completed the aspect with the slower moving planet.

An applying aspect signifies a condition in the life of the native that has not yet come into manifestation or fruition. Consequently, its effect will become evident as the native's life progresses.

A separating aspect indicates a condition where the circumstance signified by the aspect is already a part of the native's experience. Therefore, its influence will be an aftereffect of these occurrences. As the native's life progresses, this effect will become less noticeable or incorporated into the subconscious experiences of the native.

Significance of Approaching and Departing Aspects

A departing aspect occurs when the faster moving planet has already had a conjunction with the slower moving planet and is moving toward the opposition with the slower moving planet. An example of this would be a sextile between Mercury in 15 Gemini and Saturn in 15 Aries. This would be a departing sextile because the conjunction of Mercury and Saturn occurred previously in Aries and the opposition between these planets will not occur until Mercury reaches the opposite sign of Libra. Therefore, this is called a departing sextile because Mercury is departing or moving away from the conjunction of Saturn when the aspect occurs.

A departing aspect always carries a more personal and subjective quality of one of the houses or signs between Aries and Virgo, or the first house and the sixth house. In this case, the sextile will have the connotation of individual thought and communication associated with Gemini superseding the universal and intuitive concepts associated with Aquarius, which is strongly characteristic of approaching sextiles.

An approaching aspect occurs when the faster moving planet is moving away from the opposition with the slower moving planet and moving toward a conjunction with the slower moving planet. An example of this is a sextile between Mercury and Saturn in 15 Aquarius and Aries respectively. In such a case, the opposition of Mercury and Saturn occurred previously when Mercury was in Libra and the conjunction of these planets will occur when Mercury reaches Aries. In the case of the approaching sextile of Mercury and Saturn, the mental discipline indicated by this sextile is predominantly colored by the scientific and universal humanitarian qualities of Aquarius, as opposed to the more individualistic mental expressions of Gemini.

Approaching aspects have a more universal impersonal and social connotation than their departing counterparts. This is characteristic of the socially-oriented signs from Libra through Pisces and the seventh through the twelfth houses.

The important thing to consider is the basic difference between an approaching and departing aspect. The concept of approaching and departing aspects should not be confused with the concept of applying and separating aspects.

Conjunction (0 Degrees)

The conjunction, especially of the Sun, has a first house significance affecting the will and being of the native, as well as their expression. The conjunction marks a strong focalized potential for expression with a tendency toward direction, action, and self-dramatization. It strengthens the will in relation to the character of the planets in conjunction, and in relation to the houses in which the planets are placed and the houses those planets rule.

The conjunction gives emphasis to the sign and the house in which it is placed. Considered to be the most powerful of all aspects when exact or close to exact, the conjunction indicates one of the strongest psychological tendencies or traits.

The conjunction is a major aspect allowed a six degree orb for the planets and a ten degree orb when one of the lights is involved.

Opposition (180 Degrees)

The opposition is a major aspect and is allowed a six degree orb in the case of the planets and ten degrees where one of the lights is involved.

The opposition has a seventh house Venus-Saturn-Libra connotation and represents a situation in which other people are involved in the affairs ruled by the character of the two planets in the aspect and the signs and houses they affect.

The opposition aspect represents a situation of either cooperation or conflict between the psychological drives represented by the two planets making the aspect. This tendency usually externalizes itself in a relationship involving another individual with whom the native has to cooperate or separate.

Sextile (60 Degrees)

The sextile is a major aspect having an eleventh house and third house connotation. It is given a six degree orb for planets and a ten degree orb when the lights are involved. The sextile influences mental perception and represents an easy flow of thought relative to the affairs ruled by the relationship between the two planets involved.

The aspect has a combined Mercury, Saturn, and Uranus connotation. In other words, it can give the mental perception for bringing ideas into practical manifestation; it is an aspect of opportunity. Ideas must be acted upon in order to realize benefits from them. The sextile also deals with communication, groups, hopes and wishes, contracts, and writing—in short, all things that pertain to the eleventh and third houses.

If the sextile is approaching (the faster moving planet is moving *toward* the slower moving planet), the aspect has an eleventh house significance, thus giving the aspect a more scientific and simultaneously a more occult interpretation.

The approaching phase of the sextile deals with larger issues and thus has a more universal significance. Success can be brought about through cooperation with other people or groups. The door is open, as it were, to the fulfillment of one's hopes and wishes, but one must walk through this open door in order to realize the benefits of this particular aspect.

If the sextile aspect is departing (the faster moving planet is moving *away* from the slower moving planet), the aspect has a more purely intellectual third house connotation.

It takes on the coloring of whatever planets are involved in the aspect and deals essentially with thought and communication of thought. For example, Neptune in the sixth house in 20 Cancer and Mars in 22 Virgo in the eighth house could give rise to inventive ideas as to how matters relating to insurance, taxes, inheritances, and all things pertaining to the eighth house can be used to advantage in rendering the spiritual service denoted by Neptune in the sixth house. These services could also relate to health, healing, and food—all things that pertain to the sixth house.

Square (90 Degrees)

The square is a major aspect of with a six degree orb allowed except in the case of the lights, where a ten degree orb is allowed. The square is of major importance in denoting karmic difficulties and limitations; it also indicates those areas in our life where adjustments must be made and tremendous effort and work must be exerted in order to realize even minor gains.

The square has a tenth and fourth house connotation and has a combined relationship of Saturn and the Moon. (Both Saturn and the Moon deal with the habit tendencies of the past. The square denotes karmic liabilities experienced because of previous misuse of the free will.)

If the square is an approaching aspect (the faster moving planet is moving *toward* the slower moving planet), the aspect has a tenth house Saturn connotation, indicating that the native is forced in this lifetime to learn through hardship and hard work the lessons they failed to learn in previous incarnations. The square can also indicate a necessity to willingly build new experiences and abilities in order to round out undeveloped areas of the individual's experience.

If the square is a departing aspect (the faster moving planet is moving *away* from the slower moving planet), the native must correct the mistakes and wrong actions of the past or overcome bad habit tendencies that are an obstacle to the native's further development. In this case, the aspect has a fourth-house lunar connotation. In some way the foundations of the life structure must be built and improved, especially with regard to the planets, signs, and houses involved in the square.

Trine (120 Degrees)

The trine is a major aspect and is given a six degree orb in the case of the planets and a ten degree orb in the case of the lights. The trine has a fifth and ninth house connotation and a Jupiter, Sun, and Neptune significance.

The trine is an aspect of creativity and spiritual expansion. With the fifth house connotation it brings pleasure and happiness. The trine is considered to be the most fortunate and beneficent of all aspects, indicating the rewards of a past good karma to which the native is entitled. For example, a trine aspect between the Sun and Jupiter gives such protection to individuals that they can never be completely overcome.

If the trine is approaching (the faster moving planet is moving *toward* the slower moving planet), it has a ninth house Jupiter-Neptune significance and indicates the unfolding of philosophic, spiritual, and higher mental faculties. The trine gives a prophetic ability in affairs relating to the two planets that are in trine aspect, the signs and houses in which they are placed, and the houses they rule.

If the trine is departing (the faster moving planet is moving *away* from the slower moving planet), it has a fifth house, Sun-Leo significance and gives expansion and good fortune in creative self-expression and in the expression of power in the affairs ruled by the relationships of two planets, the signs, and the houses in which they are placed, the houses they rule, and the planets they dispose.

Semi-sextile (30 Degrees)

The semi-sextile is one-twelfth of a circle. It is considered one of the minor aspects and is given only a three degree orb as opposed to the six degree orb given to major aspects. If the Sun or Moon is involved in the aspect, an orb of five degrees is allowed.

The semi-sextile has a twelfth house connotation if the faster moving planet is moving *toward* the slower moving planet. The approaching aspect indicates that a condition is developing and coming to fruition that is the result of long previous experience and the process of living.

This aspect indicates the opportunity to capitalize on the resources of the unconscious mind and past experience and contacts formed over a long period of time. It represents the integration of experience into the conscious awareness of the native. The past experience is of the nature of the faster moving planet, and this experience is absorbed by the slower moving planet.

Example: Saturn in the third house and Mercury in the second house at 6 Sagittarius. Saturn in the third indicates ability in practical, concrete expression of thought. Mercury passing through the second and being neutral would suggest the use of past experience by applying the mind to problems of material resources or gains. It could be used as a means of applying this financial know-how to make possible the practical expression of the native's ideas by producing funds necessary for practical mental endeavors.

A departing semi-sextile aspect has a second house significance and therefore deals with the building up of practical resources of wherewithal to make further expansion and unfoldment possible. This aspect relates to earning money or acquiring property by one's own efforts. This aspect provides the opportunity for gain, but the natives must apply themselves in a practical way in order to realize this gain.

For example, if a native has Jupiter in the fifth house in 14 Libra and Mars is in the sixth house in 12 Scorpio, then through application of Mars energy in work and service, the native can provide the materials for an expanded and happy social life by making possible the art objects, food, entertainment, and venue to have parties and social activities. This is but one of the possible fifth house expressions. This aspect would also indicate the application of energy to creative endeavors generating wealth through that which is produced.

Decile (36 Degrees)

The decile is a minor aspect having a second and eleventh house connotation. It is an aspect of mental resourcefulness and confers insight into the inner workings of natural forces.

This aspect, along with the quintile (72 degrees), tredecile (108 degrees), and bi-quintile (144 degrees), represents one of the angles inherent in the pentagram and the pentagonal do-decahendronal matrix pattern. It therefore has an influence that is more subtle, interconnective, and occult, but effective nonetheless.

This is a minor aspect that should be limited to a two degree orb. It becomes more effective if it is part of aspect configuration involving other deciles, quintiles, tredeciles, or bi-quintiles. Its power is also enhanced if the two planets involved are part of a midpoint configuration, in parallel aspect, or in mutual reception.

If the decile is an approaching aspect—that is, if the faster moving planet is moving *toward* the slower moving planet— then it has an eleventh house scientific and occult Uranian connotation and can involve groups.

If the decile is a departing aspect—that is, if the faster moving planet is moving *away* from the slower moving planet—the

aspect has a second house Venus connotation of practical resourcefulness.

Semi-square (45 Degrees)

The semi-square is allowed only half the orb allotted for the
square, or three degrees between two planets and five degrees if
the Sun or Moon is involved.

This aspect has an eleventh and second house connotation.
It is a stress aspect indicating irritation and difficulty in getting
something established.

If the semi-square is an approaching aspect—if the faster
moving planet is moving *toward* the slower moving planet—it
has an eleventh house significance, indicating sudden upsets in
one's hopes and wishes or friendships and group endeavors. This
is because it partakes in a negative way of the nature of Saturn
and Uranus, the co-rulers of Aquarius in the eleventh house.

For example, if a person has Saturn in the tenth house in 6
Gemini and Venus in 20 Aries in the ninth house, friendships
with wealthy older women of foreign origin met on long journeys or through associations could have an irritating or adverse
effect upon the professional ambitions of the native.

If the semi-square is departing—that is, if the faster moving planet is moving *away* from the slower moving planet—the
semi-square aspect has a negative Venus second house connotation.

For example, a man has Mars in 10 Cancer in the twelfth
house semi-square Uranus in 23 Taurus. This man is an inventor
who has experienced frequent irritation and difficulty in acquiring funds for his inventions. These irritations often arise sud-
denly (Uranus) and because of secret motives or the dislike of
secret enemies (Mars in the twelfth house).

Quintile (72 Degrees)

Although the quintile is a minor aspect, it can be an important one. It has a third and tenth house connotation and is an aspect indicating special talent or genius. It confers originality and penetrating insight. It has a combined Mercury-Saturn connotation, giving the ability to express thoughts and ideas in a concrete way and to put them into structured manifestation. It is also good for mathematics and problem-solving.

If the quintile is an approaching aspect—that is, if the faster moving planet is moving *toward* the slower moving planet—the aspect has a tenth house connotation indicating genius and special talent as applied to professional ambition and unfoldment of long-range career plans and purposes.

If the quintile is a departing aspect—that is, if the faster moving planet is moving *away* from the slower moving planet—the aspect has a third house mental connotation, indicating that genius and special talent is used more for the unfoldment of mental potentialities for their own sake.

For example, if the person has the Sun in the fourth house in 12 Sagittarius and the Moon in 24 Aquarius in the sixth house, this indicates special talent in determining new methods and ideas for improving the home and rendering services in the home.

Tredecile (108 Degrees)

This is a minor aspect that theoretically should be an aspect of importance close to that of a major aspect. However, it is generally considered to be a minor aspect and is given a two degree orb.

The tredecile has a ninth house and fourth house connotation with a combined connotation of Moon-Jupiter Neptune,

It therefore has a quality of mental growth and expansion. This growth lays solid foundations for further unfoldment.

This aspect relates directly to the pentagonal-dodecahedronal matrix structure as a result of having the same angle that exists between two adjoining edges of a pentagonal-dodecahedron.

For example, if a person has Mars in the tenth house in 15 Virgo and Saturn in 3 Capricorn making a tredecile aspect, this indicates mental growth and expansion and professional ambition as a result of hard work and disciplined control of energy.

If the aspect is an approaching one—that is, if the faster moving planet is moving *toward* the slower moving planet—the aspect has a ninth house significance indicating that mental unfoldment of the higher mind is the dominating quality.

If the tredecile aspect is departing—that is, if the faster moving planet is moving *away* from the slower moving planet—the aspect has a more practical connotation of expanding the home base of operation and family relationships.

Sesquiquadrate (135 Degrees)

The sesquiquadrate is a minor aspect that has a negative, irritating fifth house and eighth house connotation. It is given a three degree orb for the planets and a five degree for the lights.

Its effect is somewhat similar to that of a semi-square. It has a combined connotation of the Sun, Mars, and Pluto, suggesting impulsiveness, over-forcefulness, liability to anger and irritation, and domineering qualities.

If the sesquiquadrate is approaching—that is, if the faster moving planet is moving *toward* the slower moving planet—the aspect has a Mars-Pluto eighth house connotation. This relates it to death, the affairs of the dead, insurance, taxes, and joint finances. It brings difficulties in these matters related to the affairs ruled by the relationship between two planets forming the aspect, the signs and houses in which they are placed, the houses they rule, and planets they disposit.

If the sesquiquadrate is formed to the ruler of the eighth house, this can be an indication of danger to the life of the individual when reinforced by other aspects with a similar connotation.

When the sesquiquadrate aspect is a departing aspect—that is, if the faster moving planet is moving *away* from the slower moving planet—the aspect has a negative Sun fifth house connotation, indicating problems in self-expression, creative endeavors, love life, relations with children, and the tendency to be domineering—in short, all things pertaining to Leo and the fifth house.

Bi-quintile (144 Degrees)

The bi-quintile is a minor aspect that is allowed a two degree orb for the planets and a three degree orb for the lights. This aspect has a combined fifth and eighth house connotation along with a combined Sun, Mars, and Pluto significance.

This is an aspect of creative, occult powers that partake of the mental nature of the quintile aspect. It can thus be associated with clairvoyance, mental perception, and magic. This is because the eighth house, which Pluto rules and where Uranus is exalted, is concerned with death and rebirth, processes of transformation and the subtle hidden forces of nature.

If the bi-quintile is an approaching aspect—that is, if the faster moving planet is moving *toward* the slower moving planet—the aspect has a Mars-Pluto-Uranus-eighth house-Scorpio significance. This indicates concern with the hidden or occult forces in relationship to the two planets involved in the aspect, the signs and houses in which they are placed, and the houses that the planets rule.

If the bi-quintile is a departing one—that is, if the faster moving planet is moving *away* from the slower moving planet—the aspect has a fifth house connotation, relating it to genius in creative self-expression concerned with the relationship of the planets involved in the aspect, the signs and houses in which they are placed, and the houses they rule.

Quincunx or Inconjunct (150 Degrees)

The inconjunct is allowed half the orb permitted for a major aspect, or three degrees for planets and five degrees if one of the lights is involved.

The inconjunct has a Virgo-sixth house-Scorpio-eighth house connotation. It requires the improvement and regeneration of existing conditions and problems through work, correct scientific method, attention to detail, and regeneration of desires. Failure to do this will result in work and health problems, destruction of existing conditions, and difficult, frustrating circumstances.

An approaching inconjunct has the significance of Scorpio, eighth house, Mars, Pluto, and Uranus. In extreme cases, approaching inconjuncts involving Mars, Pluto, Uranus, or Saturn can trigger critical circumstances involving life and death issues. The outcome of these events will have far-reaching and irrevocable consequences for good or ill. The undesirable effects of an approaching inconjunct can be avoided through regeneration of motives. Any selfish intent to use occult power or collective resources for personal advantage will bring unpleasant and sometimes dire consequences for the native. This approaching inconjunct is related to the occult and hidden forces of nature because of the Pluto co-rulership and the Uranus exaltation in Scorpio.

The departing inconjunct has the significance of Virgo, Mercury, and the sixth house. Departing inconjuncts contain the lesson of efficient work and attention to detail. Failure to heed this lesson can result in ill-health, unemployment, and subjugation to difficult and sometimes seemingly impossible circumstances caused by the ineptitude and inefficiency of others.

Vigintile (18 Degrees)

The vigintile is harmonious, with a combined twelfth and first house influence. It deals with the culmination of old conditions and the creation of new ones. It is associated with Jupiter, Neptune, Pisces, Mars, Aries, and Pluto. The native is able to draw upon accumulated past experiences represented by Neptune and Pisces. It also gives the ability to initiate new and better beginnings represented by Mars, Aries, and Pluto.

The approaching vigintile aspect occurs when the faster moving planet is moving *toward* a conjunction with the slower moving planet. It represents a preparatory stage for launching a new phase of self-expression. During this phase the native gathers past experiences and resources and assesses the way in which he or she will make a new start in the light of these factors.

The departing vigintile has a predominantly Aries connotation and creates favorable or harmonious circumstances for launching a new phase of self-expression. It occurs when the faster moving planet is moving *away* from the conjunction with the slower moving planet.

Parallel

Two planets are in parallel if they have the same declination within a one degree orb. Declination is defined as a planet's distance in degrees and minutes from the celestial equator. The declinations of the planets are given in some ephemerides.

If both planets involved in a parallel aspect are north of the celestial equator or if both planets have southern declination or are south of the equator, then the parallel aspect acts like a conjunction. However, if one of the planets has a northern declination and the other planet has a southern declination, then the parallel aspect acts like an opposition.

If another aspect exists between two planets in parallel, the nature of this aspect is rendered twice as powerful by virtue of the two planets also being in parallel aspect.

For example, a sextile exists between Venus and Uranus, and Venus and Uranus are also in parallel aspect.

Instead of the individual having the opportunity to develop talent in original artistic creativity and at times being electrified with charm, these attributes become a major distinguishing characteristic of the native.

CHAPTER FOUR

Ladder of the Planets

There is much controversy in current astrological thought regarding the correct planetary sign rulership and exaltation of the outer planets, Uranus, Neptune, and Pluto. All things in the universe follow natural laws of order and structure. Therefore, there is a coherent pattern that explains the rulership of these outer planets, as well as the seven traditional planets.

The Astrological Mandala of Sign Rulerships

The use of geometric patterns for mandalas to describe astrological relationships is common. We are all familiar with the modes of expression: the elements and the groupings of masculine, feminine, positive, and negative signs. Each planet rules a masculine, positive sign and a feminine, negative sign, and thus the principle of each planet expresses through an active, initiatory phase and a passive, receptive phase.

With so much controversy regarding the sign rulerships of the trans-Saturnian planets, namely Uranus, Neptune, and Pluto, the use of mandalas could prove to be a valuable technique in understanding these rulerships and the insights they give. The ladder of the planets is an old astrological tradition that existed in medieval times prior to the discovery of Uranus, Neptune, and Pluto.

The ladder of the planets is the organization of the signs of the zodiac into six pairs. Each pair of signs is ruled by the same planet or planets. The first rung of the ladder is Cancer and Leo, ruled by the Sun and the Moon. The second rung of the ladder is Gemini and Virgo, ruled by Mercury. The third rung of the ladder Taurus and Libra, ruled by Venus. The fourth rung of the ladder is Aries and Scorpio, ruled by Mars. The fifth rung of the ladder is Sagittarius and Pisces, ruled by Jupiter. The sixth rung of the ladder is Capricorn and Aquarius, ruled by Saturn.

Trans-Saturnian Planets

Thus far we have described the traditional planetary rulerships of early astrology without including Uranus, Neptune, and Pluto. Now we will examine how these trans-Saturnian planets are integrated into this ladder. We are proposing that Uranus is a higher octave ruler of Capricorn and Aquarius and that Neptune is a higher octave ruler of Sagittarius and Pisces. Pluto is the higher octave ruler of Aries and Scorpio. We are, in effect, coming down the ladder with the higher octave rulers or trans-Saturnian planets.

Some of these rulerships, upon superficial examination, may seem inappropriate, particularly Uranus' co-rulership of Capricorn. Saturn's rulership of Capricorn includes corporate structures, industry, government, and established organizations. If Uranus represents reformist tendencies, the new age consciousness and departure from the traditional, how then can Uranus be co-ruler of traditional, conservative Capricorn? This question arises because there is much that is not properly understood about Uranus.

Alice Bailey wrote that Uranus is a seventh ray planet. The seventh ray rules the physical plane, including its higher etheric sub-planes and the seventh or lowest sub-plane of each of the other six planes. Consequently, Uranus rules the process by which any phenomenon comes into or goes out of objective, physical manifestation.

To the average individual who does not understand the laws of precipitation, this process seems mysterious, occult, and sudden. Uranus has the reputation of operating in a sudden, unexplainable way. Once one has gained the clairvoyant vision to know the thought-form in the more subtle, etheric dimensions that organize physical plane events and substance through the process of harmonic reflections, Uranus no longer seems mysterious or inexplicable.

Capricorn as an earth sign deals with the organization and management of physical plane resources and affairs. Capricorn as a cardinal sign has a very dynamic and aggressive side to its nature as shown by the exaltation of Mars in Capricorn. Saturn's function in Capricorn is to organize and plan an effective course of action. It should not be surprising that Uranus, planet of dynamic change, should have a place in Capricorn. Mars, which is exalted in Capricorn is a co-ruler of Scorpio where Uranus is exalted. The exaltation of Uranus in Scorpio is descriptive of the simultaneous destruction and creation of physical form manifestations. This operates according to the occult law of liberation whereby old, outmoded forms are destroyed so that the indwelling consciousness or potential can be released to embody a new and more highly evolved form which is more in keeping with the needs of the indwelling, evolving life.

The sign of a planet's exaltation rules the process whereby the planet derives its basic function. It is, therefore, appropriate that Uranus, planet of dynamic change, is exalted in Scorpio, the sign of fundamental transformation and transmutation, death and rebirth.

The sign of a planet's rulership indicates the ways or methods through which the planet most readily expresses the basic, functional principles that originated in the sign of its exaltation.

Capricorn rules established governmental business and economic institutions that are the instigators of much change and innovation. Uranus rules the physical plane manifestation of subtle forces such as electricity and its use in all phases of modern technology.

Scientific research in the fields of electronics, atomic energy, space exploration, etc., come under the rulership of Uranus. It is obvious that government and big business are responsible for funding and carrying out most of this research and technological innovation, paid for by taxes and corporate funds ruled by Scorpio, where Uranus is exalted.

Uranus, like Saturn, has much to do with the principle of organization. Matter has its origin in the organization of vibration. Form and structure exist only because of organization—thus the strong link between Uranus and Saturn. Saturn is said to be the prerequisite of Uranus because self-discipline is essential before true freedom can be realized. Saturn rules the process of building specific, mental patterns of thought-forms that provide the mental mold for the organization of energy into physical manifestation through the precipitating influence of Uranus energy. In human terms the principle of organization expresses itself in group and organizational activities. This group process is ruled by Aquarius, of which Uranus is the higher octave ruler in the ladder of planets.

Aquarius, which is a positive, masculine air sign, is more concerned with intellectual thought processes and the formulation of ideas around which group activities can be coordinated. Aquarius provides the initial positive force of intellectual conceptualization which is then expressed in a concrete way through practical, Capricorn, organized business activities. Capricorn, which is a negative, feminine, receptive earth sign, receives the innovative ideas of Aquarius, institutionalizes them, and brings them into objective material manifestation.

In astrology Uranus rules creative, intuitively inspired ideas that are new and revolutionary in terms of the established modes of behavior. This concept is most easily associated with the freedom loving, positive, masculine, intellectual sign Aquarius. Success in business or professional affairs, ruled by Capricorn, can also depend on intuitive insight and innovative action involving the cardinality of Capricorn.

Neptune in the ladder of the planets is the higher octave co-ruler of Sagittarius, as well as Pisces. Neptune is ruler of the imagination, literally image-ation, the picture making faculty of the mind. As such, it deals with dreams, memories of the past, the subconscious mind, and its deep-seated, psychological habit patterns.

Neptune also deals with dreams, ideals, and hopes for the future. Neptune rules extended clairvoyant and clairaudient faculties of perception. Consequently, it is associated with religious and mystical experiences, and on the negative side with hallucinations and psychotic phenomena.

Sagittarius is the sign traditionally associated with religion, philosophy, and higher education. Most religions began with the mystical experiences of an inspired teacher or prophet and later became institutionalized in a typically Jupiter way.

Religious art posters and more lyrical forms of music have become popular in contrast to Neptune in Scorpio which gave us the chaotic acid rock era.

Sagittarius is a sign of aiming at a mark or goal or future ideal. Neptune provides the imaginative faculty for the formation of future goals and ideals.

In traditional astrology, Neptune is well-known as a co-ruler of Pisces. The reasons are fairly obvious since Pisces deals with the subconscious mind, seclusion, asylums, monasteries, ashrams, and places of meditation and spiritual retreat. Pisces is a highly intuitive, mystical sign synchronized with the highly imaginative faculties associated with Neptune. Pisces is also a highly artistic sign, in keeping with the creative imagination that the Neptunian faculties make possible. Pisces is highly emotional and sensitive on a subconscious, if not a conscious, level. This makes them telepathically aware of all the subtle nuances of their environment and the people in it. Neptune is exalted in Cancer, which rules the family conditioning and early childhood environment where basic subconscious attitudes are formed. Cancer also relates to the deep-seated roots of consciousness that originate in the karmic past, which is ruled by Neptune.

Pluto is the higher octave ruler of Aries and Scorpio, and has much to do with the Kundalini energy or sex force. Scorpio is the astrological sign usually ascribed to Pluto; it rules the sex energy related to the lowest chakra center at the base of the spine. When the kundalini or spinal spirit fire is raised from the bottom chakra or center to the highest head center or thousand petal lotus, as it is called, a major initiation into enlightened consciousness takes place. These two centers are related to Scorpio and Aries, respectively, Scorpio ruling the generative organs and Aries ruling the head. These two centers act like the positive and negative poles of a magnet and relate to the power or will aspect of being. Pluto as ruler of Scorpio and Aries relates to the cycle of death and rebirth or one of a new beginning.

Scorpio is the sign usually associated with death and Aries is the sign associated with new beginnings or birth. Thus we have the negative Scorpio expression of this energy and the Aries positive expression of the same power. We use the words positive and negative in the sense of polarity only, with no moral connotation since no sign is inherently more spiritual than another.

The Aries-Scorpio rung of the ladder deals with the use of energy or power. However, there are different kinds of energy and power. In most cases human action is based on the desire principle of Mars rather than a true expression of a mental decision based on impartial principles and a spiritual expression of will. The desire principle is ruled by Mars, the lower octave ruler of Aries and Scorpio. Only in advanced people is the Pluto expression of will brought into play.

The Pluto principle deals with the faculty of attention itself, whereby one consciously or subconsciously selects the thoughts entertained by the mind. Since everything originates in thought, each individual creates his or her own destiny according to his other choice of thoughts. Conscious, purposeful choice of thoughts requires an exercise of the spiritual will and of the principle of awareness. This ability to watch the mind think and thus be able to monitor it and decide what thoughts should be allowed to be entertained by the mind comes under the rulership of Pluto and constitutes man's capacity to regenerate and remake himself and his destiny. It is the individual's opportunity to become a true spiritual being if he or she so wills. Only by wisely choosing the thoughts that will be allowed to pass the discriminating bar of the mind and using the Mars principle of desire and action to transform these constructive thoughts into concrete expression can mankind's higher aspirations become a reality.

Basic universal substance or energy can neither be created nor destroyed, but its form manifestation can be transformed from one manifestation to another. Any inharmonious use of universal energy must eventually be transformed into a constructive expression. It cannot be permanently pushed aside or ignored without damaging the ongoing process of life. This is a universal law and applies at all levels, biological, ecological, industrial, psychological, and spiritual.

At the present time we are dealing with an ecological problem of such vast proportions that it is becoming a threat to the survival of mankind and life on earth; and all because this basic law of recycling has been ignored. There are no garbage cans in the universe, no place where waste products can be pushed aside permanently and forgotten. Unless mankind recognizes and effectively deals with this truth, we are all doomed to extinction. We can no longer afford short-sighted, economic greed that has no concern for the survival of future generations.

On the psychological level, neuroses and psychoses are brought about by a failure to properly transmute and redirect the psychic energy locked up in emotional memories and habit patterns of the past. Pluto in its rulership of Scorpio deals with the process of bringing anything to an end or conclusion when it has outlived its usefulness, so that its energy and substance can be used over in a new and useful manifestation.

One of the greatest secrets of successful living is knowing when and how to end something. Without proper death, there can be no new birth or life. Death and birth are two sides of the same process in which neither can exist without the other. What is destroyed and recreated is only the form manifestation. The basic essence of which all form manifestations are built is eternal and immutable; it can neither be created nor destroyed. It is!

The full experiential realization of this truth is one of the greatest initiations on the path of spiritual enfoldment and it is ruled by Pluto, Aries, and Scorpio.

The process of redistribution of psychic energy is ruled by Pluto, while Mars rules the practical, physical action that makes this possible, thus giving the person a new start represented by Aries. Aries and the first house rule the self, the basic self-aware principle in man.

Through the Pluto experience, the individual must go through the ultimate confrontation with the self and come to terms with his or her own spiritual essence. Pluto is a hard taskmaster and brooks no superficiality or avoidance of life's basic issues and fundamental laws. His message is regenerate or die; there is no choice.

Pluto is exalted in Leo, the sign of focalized energy or will. The Sun, which rules Leo, is a cosmic focalization of primal energy represented by the Sun's exaltation in Aries. Through the concentration of this energy as represented by Leo, creative activity is born, thus making possible the origin of Pluto's principle of transmutation and transformation. Through the concentration of this universal energy, harmonic interfaces and interchanges are created between higher and lower dimensions. This law makes possible a radical transformation of consciousness ruled by Pluto. Thus Pluto gains its power in Leo and expresses it through the transforming activities of Scorpio and Aries.

The First Rung of the Ladder of the Planets

The first rung of the ladder of planets consists of Cancer and Leo. It is the Sun rung of the ladder because the Moon, which rules Cancer, is only a passive reflector of solar energy and has no life of its own.

According to esoteric astrology, the Moon is a dead planet that veils the Sun, Uranus, and Vulcan. The Moon as ruler of Cancer represents the passive or receptive phase of the Sun principle. This energy is potent in its passive phase because Cancer is a cardinal sign of immediate action or response.

The positive, dynamic phase of the solar energy is expressed through Leo. The intensity, authority and dynamism of the Leo personality is well known. Through Leo the solar energy gives birth to the creation of progeny on all levels of manifestation.

The feminine Cancer phase of the solar energy nurtures and mothers growing life forms, providing physical sustenance for their bodies.

The Moon, which acts as the intermediary of this feminine aspect of the solar energy, is exalted in Taurus, a fixed, primal, earth sign providing the physical substance that the Moon molds into growing life forms. Thus the Moon derives her function through the sign Taurus. The Moon's function is expressed most readily through the sign Cancer, which rules parenthood, home, family life, and the nurturing of the young. The Sun being the central focus of life in the solar system must derive its power from a greater source, which is the universal cosmic energy represented by the sign Aries, the sign of primal energy.

The Second Rung of the Ladder of the Planets

The second rung of the ladder of the planets consists of Gemini and Virgo, ruled by Mercury. The creative activity of the solar energy must be guided by intelligence. Mercury rules the ability to perceive, learn, adapt, and communicate, thus giving the ability to assimilate, absorb, use, and communicate information. In Gemini, Mercury gives the ability to rationally trace out the cause and effect relationship of that which is experienced in the environment. In Virgo this knowledge and experience is applied through work for the providing of physical necessities and the maintenance of health and well-being.

The experience of work with its trial and error provides a valuable learning experience. It equips one for even greater accomplishments. This also gives man the dignity of participating by carrying forward the creative process begun in Leo. Virgo provides the continuation and refinement of this process.

Mercury is exalted in Aquarius. The ability of the individual mind to perceive, think, and communicate is derived from the universal ocean of cosmic energy because all intelligence is a patterning of energy. Aquarius rules the universal superconscious mind in which the individual mind ruled by Mercury exists and out of which it is formed.

The Third Rung of the Ladder of the Planets

The third rung of the ladder of the planets consists of Taurus and Libra, ruled by Venus. Energy and intelligence alone are not sufficient for life's further development without social relatedness and cooperation ruled by Venus. All beauty arises out of the harmonious organization of the component parts of that which is beautiful. This applies in art, music, architecture, and human relationships, as well as to physical beauty. This harmonious relationship necessitates justice and an exchange of give and take as indicated by the rulership of Venus by Libra. This in turn can manifest as beauty of form indicated in Venus' rulership of Taurus, an earth sign.

Venus rules money, which is a medium of exchange in economic relationships.

The exaltation of Venus in Pisces indicates the ability to cooperate which arises from compassion and understanding born out of the experience of the previous signs of the zodiac.

Harmonious relationships are the expression of life that makes possible marriage and other forms of partnership, as well as mutually benefitting, business exchange.

The Fourth Rung of the Ladder of the Planets

The fourth rung of the ladder of the planets consists of Aries and Scorpio. The lower octave ruler of these signs is Mars, which rules the desire principle leading to action in Aries and efforts at self-regeneration in Scorpio. Mars rules the sex drive, which is nature's insurance of continuing rebirth to replace death. If the Mars principle of Aries is misused, it leads to self-centered aggression, expressing as a tendency to ride roughshod over others.

In Scorpio this selfish aggression leads to selfish appropriations of collective resources for personal aggrandizement. This economic selfishness, wanting to control more than one's share of resources, is the basis of most wars and conflicts throughout history. The negative expression of the Mars-Scorpio energy manifests as greed and uncontrolled sexual passion. If the Mars energy is guided by intelligence, wisdom, love, and the spiritual will, it will lead to constructive action and practical accomplishment as revealed by its exaltation in Capricorn.

Mars' exaltation in Capricorn demonstrates that action based on desire, which is ruled by Mars, arises out of the necessity to conquer and control material plane circumstances in order to find security in them. The most useful place for the expression of Mars energy is in building a profession or place in the world ruled by Capricorn, an earth sign.

The Fifth Rung of the Ladder of the Planets

The fifth rung of the ladder of the planets consists of Sagittarius and Pisces. Jupiter is the lower octave ruler of these signs, and Sagittarius rules all codifications of collective, cultural thought. These can take many forms, such as religions, philosophies, cultural traditions, social mores, law, and higher education, as well as the institutions that represent these things. These traditions and institutions arise out of a need for social harmony and harmonious cooperation that make possible peace, well being, and security for the populace.

There are collective needs of society beyond the capacity of a single individual to handle. Therefore, systems and institutions of social cooperation, law, and justice arise to pool collective energy and resources to meet common, collective needs. This process is ruled by benevolent Jupiter, which is a second ray planet embodying the love-wisdom aspect of consciousness. The more civilized and cultured man becomes, the more strongly this Jupiter force manifests. It would appear obvious that Jupiter rules Sagittarius, sign of the higher mind and social conscience.

Jupiter co-rules Pisces and Pisces rules hospitals, asylums, ashrams, monasteries and collective charitable institutions.

Pisces is a sign of sympathy, compassion, and understanding—qualities gained after much social experience. Jupiter is exalted in Cancer, sign of the home and family life. Cultural conditionings and social attitudes of any person originate in family upbringing and early childhood conditioning, which is ruled by Cancer. Hence, the Jupiter principle of social awareness derives its function from its exaltation sign Cancer.

The Sixth Rung of the Ladder of the Planets

The sixth rung of the ladder of the planets consists of Capricorn and Aquarius. Saturn is the lower octave ruler of these signs and expresses the principle of organization and discipline and the necessary limitations for practical accomplishments. This organizing, structure-building principle functions in Capricorn as business and governmental organization. Capricorn also rules the personal discipline required for success in one's profession. Discipline is imposed on the individual by the law and rules of the established governmental and social institutions. The individual must learn to work and build within these limits and laws. Should these laws become crystallized or outmoded, habit-breaking Uranus energy will bring about necessary changes.

In Aquarius, the Saturn principle brings about organization through intelligent, coordinated group work, and cooperation. Through a developed attention span or steady mental concentration it is possible to establish a harmonic link with the universal consciousness, thereby allowing the Uranus faculty of intuition to operate.

Aquarius rules friends, people with whom we work and share goals and objectives. The Saturn aspect of Aquarius represents the work and organized cooperation needed to attain these goals and objectives. Libra is the sign of relationships between the self and others, and through the reactions of others, one is forced to experience the consequences of his or her actions, thus bringing the principle of karma or cause and effect into play. Out of this interaction in relationships, ruled by Libra, duties and responsibilities arise, giving birth to the principle of Saturn through its exaltation in Libra.

Saturn's exaltation in Libra, an air sign and its co-rulership of Aquarius, also an air sign, indicates that Saturn is a highly intellectual planet. This should not be surprising since all true organization begins in the mind. This later manifests on the physical plane through the earth sign Capricorn. Saturn is a third ray planet that expresses as active intelligence leading to form manifestation.

This mandala is a coherent system showing the relationship of astrological rulerships in their progression from one stage to another.

www.ingramcontent.com/pod-product-compliance
Lightning Source LLC
LaVergne TN
LVHW091229080426
835509LV00009B/1223